Pitmen Painters

William Feaver

PITMEN
PAINTERS

The Ashington Group
1934–1984

Mid Northumberland Arts Group
Carcanet Press
1993

To the Ashington Group

First published in paperback in 1993 by Mid Northumberland Arts Group
Ashington, Northumberland NE63 9XL *and*
Carcanet Press Limited
208–212 Corn Exchange Buildings, Manchester M4 3BQ

Published in hardback in 1988 by
Chatto & Windus Ltd

All rights reserved. No part of this publication may be
reproduced, stored in a retrieval system, or transmitted in any
form, or by any means, electronic, mechanical, photocopying,
recording or otherwise, without the prior permission of the
publisher.

A CIP catalogue record for this book is available from the
British Library

ISBN 0 904790 81 9 (MidNAG)
ISBN 1 85754 036 0 (Carcanet)

Copyright © William Feaver 1988, 1993

The right of William Feaver to be identified as the author of
the work has been asserted by him in accordance with the
Copyright, Designs and Patents Act of 1988.

The Publishers acknowledge the financial support of the
Arts Council of Great Britain and Northern Arts.

Printed and bound in Great Britain by
Butler & Tanner Ltd, Frome and London

Contents

Rough work, honourable or not, takes the life out of us; and the man who has been heaving clay out of a ditch all day, or driving an express train against the north wind all night, or holding a collier's helm in a gale on a lee shore, or whirling white-hot iron at a furnace mouth, is not the same man at the end of his day, or night, as one who has been sitting in a quiet room, with everything comfortable about him, reading books, or classing butterflies, or painting pictures.

JOHN RUSKIN *The Crown of Wild Olive*

I

I don't talk about art: I paint art if possible

JIMMY FLOYD

In 1934 a book was published called *A Stepladder to Painting*. In it the would-be artist was told how best to tackle every sort of subject: 'Miners Coming Back from Work in the Dusk', for example. 'To get the utmost emotional effect you would paint your miners with simple lines, merged masses, dim colours . . .'

The author, Jan Gordon, never imagined that such people could be among those he was addressing. The viewpoint, he assumed, could only be that of an outsider, studying the merged masses. 'Let us imagine that you *actually* saw your miners returning home in the broad sunlight. Now the question is: are you going to stick to the simple problem of the miners' fatigue, their desire for rest, and their exhaustion, or are you going to give expression to the irony of the men coming out of the darkness to be welcomed by the sunlight which they cannot really enjoy?'[1]

It was George Orwell's viewpoint too: 'To a Southerner, new to the mining districts, the spectacle of a shift of several hundred miners streaming out of the pit is strange and slightly sinister,' he wrote. 'Their exhausted faces, with the grime clinging in all the hollows, have a fierce, wild look.' What Orwell describes in *The Road to Wigan Pier* was photographed by Bill Brandt for his pictorial survey *The English At Home* published a year earlier, in 1936. Seven Welsh miners, as black as Al Jolsons, eyes and teeth glinting, are caught in a splash of sunshine as they reach the surface and wait to be released from the cage. Opposite them, on the facing page, three children stare from a basement window, trapped at pavement level. Miners and slum-dwellers, Brandt implies, suffer the same deprivation. The glow of a safety lamp, faint in daylight, and the whiteness of the milkjug held out by one child in mute plea signify hope or longing.

Eight years after the publication of *A Stepladder to Painting* Jan Gordon found himself writing the catalogue introduction for a London exhibition of work by the Ashington Group. The mining subjects,

OPPOSITE AND ABOVE Bill Brandt, *The English At Home*, 1936

Oliver Kilbourn, *The Off Shift*, 1937

handled by miners themselves, bore little relation to the approach he had recommended. Now he talked about 'experiences drawn from the heart, instinctively couched in appropriate mediums, expressive to a remarkable degree of understanding, candour and sincerity'. Called upon to expand on this for *Everybody's* magazine, he filled one or two of the gaps in his 'stepladder' advice.

'The art student is always thinking about what he has been taught; drawing, rules of composition and so on. Often he forgets that he has to *express* something. Often he paints just an "art" subject, because it is the right sort of thing to do. But nothing of the kind for the miners of Ashington. They have learned that what matters is the inner feeling of the thing, and they have learned to paint by the feeling.

'Effects which make us share emotions in such vivid ways cannot be taught in art schools, but the Ashington method seems somehow to conquer obstacles to expression in a curiously stimulating way.'[2]

The *Everybody's* article appeared the very month that Robert Lyon, the Ashington Group's tutor for the previous eight years, left

Harry Wilson, *The Two Shifts*, 1937

Newcastle. For Lyon those eight years had been a period of 'experiment in art appreciation', an experiment that for him as an art educationalist had succeeded beyond all expectation. Indeed he had recently produced a thesis on the subject: 'The Appreciation of Art Through the Visual and Practical Approach'.

Among the works illustrated in his thesis were Oliver Kilbourn's *The Off Shift* and Harry Wilson's *The Two Shifts*. Wilson wasn't a miner; his picture of one shift leaving the pithead while others, clean and alert, wait to descend, is that of an informed bystander.

'No amount of information or collection of notes could convey the feeling which Wilson gets into his picture', Robert Lyon wrote. 'It is the result of many years' association with the scene and with the men who go to make up that scene. He knows how quickly the groups break up on coming to the surface; nothing matters much except to get washed, changed and fed. There is no chatter and nothing casual about them as there is in the make-up of the group going on duty, but just one set purpose, to get away. Oliver Kilbourn in his treatment of the same subject, *The Off Shift*, sees it rather differently, and as he is a member of these working groups that accounts for the more personal quality of the picture. There is an almost complete lack of feeling about this design, and he himself admits this, because it has never occurred to him that there is anything more in the subject than an everyday job. He has illustrated the scene from information which is his stock-in-hand; but it leaves him entirely unmoved for he does not see the subject as a spectator in the manner of Wilson.'[3]

The 'Visual' and the 'Practical': in Lyon's thesis and in the paintings themselves a sort of realism is proclaimed; not social realism or would-be objective realism but the realism that goes with everyday acquaintance. In *Everybody's* Jan Gordon declared them 'the undoubted fine flower of Ashington culture', which struck them as a bit effusive. To the Group, painting was a form of exercise. 'From the very beginning', said Oliver Kilbourn, 'one of the reasons the class remained so was that we hadn't any desire really to become artists. That was entirely foreign to our way of thinking.'

When, in October 1934, Robert Lyon – Master of Painting at Armstrong College, then part of Durham University – first went to Ashington to run an extra-mural class, he found himself in a situation where none of the norms of art education applied.

'I was invited to join in with a number of men in Ashington who had met to discuss the possibility of forming an art appreciation group in that district. These men were by no means strangers to each other for they were all associated with the pits and had direct connection with the life of Ashington.'[4]

That life was peculiarly circumscribed. Killingworth, Dudley, Burradon, Seghill, Cramlington, Bedlington: almost every village between Newcastle and Ashington had its colliery, its rows of 'brick boxes with slate lids', as someone once described them in the *Ashington Advertiser*, and grey pitheads hunched over houses and fields. Ashington, lying between Morpeth, the county town, and Newbiggin-by-the-Sea, was a creation of the Ashington Coal Company. Rows First to Sixth were built in the 1870s. Subsequently, as the terraced grid spread, streets were named after trees and Shakespeare characters. The 1937 *Shell Guide to Northumberland & Durham* wrote the place off:

'*Ashington*: Pop. 40,000. Mining town, mostly built in the early part of this century. Dreary rows a mile long. Ashpits and mines down the middle of still unmade streets.'

There was more to it than that. Oliver Kilbourn, born in Chestnut Street in 1904, remembers how even at the worst time, around 1928 when he was on the dole for twelve months, 'activities sprang up. The Ashington Coal Company introduced the Welfare, which I think was one of the first in the country. They got two fields and made football pitches and cricket pitches and formed leagues for junior and senior football and we played to our hearts' content.'[5] The football ground doubled as a greyhound track.

'When I came here in '26 there was very little provided by the community itself', Harry Wilson said. 'There was no public library, no one here could get the loan of a book. The hospital was a small affair run by the miners themselves. There was no higher education except a small college run by the mine, for mining training. There was no grammar school or technical school.

'But I remember a philosophical society used to meet in the Council Chambers and debate the questions of the day. That was led by a person who had come from the lead mines in Cumberland: Chester Armstrong. He'd written a book called *Pilgrimage From Nenthead*. He set himself up as a sociologist and brought lectures in from all over and there were some quite good debates. Then there was the Harmonic Hall, built by the miners to encourage the string bands and the brass bands. I remember a children's orchestra, violins for about eighty kiddies, which was a feature. And we got the Bach Choir out from Newcastle and filled the Central Hall with over two thousand people on a Sunday afternoon.'

The Workers' Educational Association, advertised as 'a Federation of over 2500 Organisations, linking labour with learning', was exactly what Harry Wilson needed. 'Founded in 1903 it has grown steadily and in 1926–7 over 70,000 people took advantage of its lectures and courses. *An enquiring mind is sufficient qualification.*'[6]

'The first year I was in Ashington I was going down the main street and looked in a shop window and there was an advert for a WEA lecture on Evolution, right from start to finish. So I joined up with that.'

He could have opted for Music, Drama or Elocution, but 'Experimental Evolution' was more his line. Oliver Kilbourn was also in this class: 'We used to go into the country looking in ponds and one thing and another, for biology subjects, and we used to seek such things as flints. There's a desire in all pitmen I think to learn a little bit more than what they were taught in school.'

Wilson had been gassed in the War and, unfit to be a miner, had become a dental mechanic. 'Except for the person I worked for I had had no friends in Ashington but in the WEA I soon found myself among friends. In fact by the next year I was secretary of it. That gave me an opportunity to influence some of the things I was interested in and that was how we developed for about seven years. Biology, geology and the rest of it: it was a very very interesting class and when that finished we felt we were at a dead end again so we started on Art.'[7]

Art Class

Name	Address	29/10/34	5/11/34	12/11/34	Occupation
Brown G W. 34 Park R.		1	1	1	Joiner.
Wm Patteson	144 Sycamore St.	1	1	1	Deputy.
J J Dixon	28-9th Row	1	1	1	Filler.
A Rankin	11 North View	1	1	1	Innkeeper
J Younger	67 North Seaton Rd.	—	1	—	
G Rowe	23, Kenilworth Rd	1	1	—	Elem teacher
Wy. Young	64 poplar 25 Arundel	1	1	1	Mechanic
A F Whinnom	22 Ridsdale Sq	1	1	1	Clerk
H L Wilson	34 Station Rd.	1	1	1	Dental mechanic
J W Lillie	132 Woodhorn Rd	—	—		
Edwin Harrison	2 Bothal Terrace	—	1		
Alb. Smith	55 Beatrice St	—	1		
Roland Whinnom	13 Rutland St	—	1		
Wm Cain	Melburn Rd	—	1		
Len Morris	1 Terret Row Guston	—	1		
Thos Brownrigg	19 Langwell Cres	1	1	1	Elem teacher
Geo. Brownrigg	19	1	1	1	Filler.
Jan Ward					
L. Ross.	12 Marsh's Houses	1	1	1	Elem. Teacher
J W Beresford	30 Alexandra Rd West Sleekburn	1	—	1	Unemployed.
Peter Jackson	60 Seventh Row	1	—	—	
Jas. Floyd	149 Pont	—	1	1	Mining
Jos. Finlay	5 Fourth Row Ashington	—	1	1	Miner
R.K. Crook	16 Ninth Row Ashington	—	1	—	Gardener
J. Beal	25 Park Rd East	—	1	1	Unemployed
H. Wright	8 Park Rd.	—	1	1	Elem Teacher
Geo. Beal.	25 Park Rd	—	1	1	Elect.
Wm. Scott Armstrong	45 Coronation Ave Ashington	—	1	1	Electric welder
Alan Armstrong	58 Wansbeck Ave	—	1	1	Fitter.
T. Blenkinsop	4 Fenham Rd Lynemouth	—	1	1	Unemployed
Wm J Dobson	139 Bothal Ave Pegswood	—	1	1	Dehos Solicitor
J. R. Dobson	306 Welbeck Ave	—	1	1	Brick worker
Jas Harvey	267 Hawthorn Rd Ash.	—	1	1	Joiner.
O.G. Millbourn	61 Garden City Vello.	—	1	1	Miner.
G. Wood	East Lehork				
And Foreman	87 Rawleggen Rd c/o H Wright Park Road Ashington				

Please return
(one copy)

2

This is how it happened!
Twelve months ago I had no particular interest in Art.
Today, Art Appreciation is an essential thrill of my life.

HARRY WILSON '*Mine*', February 1936

First things first with the WEA: names and numbers. Of the thirty-eight names listed on the piece of paper that served as a register, thirteen were present at the initial meeting on 29 October 1934 in the Ashington YMCA hall, twenty-four the following week and twenty-three on 11 November. George Brown, an elderly colliery joiner and ardent antiquarian, who had been the senior figure in the Evolution class, headed the roll. Most knew each other, as pitmen, neighbours, chapel-goers, members of the ILP or from previous WEA courses.

'About twenty-four started in the group, and there were two girls,' said Harry Wilson, talking in 1971. 'Whether we were a bit robust for them I couldn't say, but they didn't last long. They came to about six lectures and since then we haven't encouraged women to come. It's a thing about the mining districts. There's a sort of strict understanding of where women fit in and where men fit in, though that's now breaking down, with women now admitted to the social clubs, which they never were.'[1]

Normal practice at evening classes was to sit in rows listening to the tutor. 'When Lyon arrived,' Oliver Kilbourn said, 'he started by giving us lectures illustrated by black and white slides on an old-fashioned lantern. These were mainly of Renaissance paintings and either religious or mythological subjects. As we didn't then know the Greek myths we were rather baffled and didn't really get anywhere with this.'

Robert Lyon ARCA was equally baffled. The Masaccios and Michelangelos he had marvelled at in Florence with Eric Ravilious and Henry ('Harry') Moore during his term as a Rome Scholar, were more or less meaningless in Ashington. Harry Youngs (mechanic), Jas. Floyd (miner), T. Beal (unemployed) and even Andy Foreman (teacher) showed no feeling for the dingy images let alone understanding. The dialect was also a problem. Besides, as he explained in the December 1935 issue of the WEA magazine, *The Highway*, 'it was perfectly

Members of the WEA Art
Class, 1934

obvious that these men had decided views on what they did not want the class to be.'

'They did not want to be told what was the correct thing to look for in a work of Art but to see for themselves why this should be correct; in other words they wanted a way, if possible, of seeing for themselves.'[2]

Within a couple of sessions Lyon came up with an alternative to what he called the 'contemplative method': a 'specially devised course of class instruction on how to draw and paint'. But this was a potential breach of WEA practice. 'At that time,' Harry Wilson recalled, 'the WEA was all theory: nothing which could possibly be interpreted as being of any use for making a living could be taught. Only those things which were cultural which meant words. Therefore one thing that Robert Lyon had to get over when he conceived what we wanted was to get permission. I don't know how he got round it, but he did.'

By quickly wrapping his inspiration in visual-and-practical-approach theory Lyon disposed of every objection. The lectures were dropped; the class became a regular body, twenty-two in number; the Old Masters were set aside for the time being and interest quickened.

It made sense to begin with lino-cutting. Lyon reckoned the men would feel less self-conscious gouging away with pocket knives than if they were set painting immediately. There were bound to be striking results, for lino-cuts are almost unavoidably emblematic. 'The selection of subject-matter was left to the individual student, and it was readily appreciated by the class that the limitations of this particular medium called for some idea which would be capable of a simpler treatment. They could appreciate, too, the restraint imposed by the medium, and the fact that simple massing and the use of the engraved line form the only means of expression.'[3]

Harry Wilson, Linocut, *c.*1934

Robert Lyon

Among the surviving prints from their first exercises, Harry Wilson's device of a miner chained to the attributes of his labour is a demonstration of what Wilson later described as 'the freedom of making designs from images and shapes developed in the mind alone and later "dressed up" to look real'. Another engraving, less preconceived but even more expressive of the way they got stuck in, so to speak, shows a miner burrowing into the coal-face; getting coal and hewing the lino are made one and the same.

Later the Group tried engraving on wood and bakelite, learning that all sorts of materials will serve and that style is largely determined by the medium used. By the third of the first series of eighteen sessions the Group had begun to define its concerns. The lino-cutting was a means of translating basic ideas into clear aims. The works could be done in class-time or at odd moments during the week; the next step however demanded more application.

Lyon, writing about his 'Experiment in Art Appreciation' for *The Listener* the following May, was keen to emphasise that the whole venture was carefully planned. 'Experiments were executed in tempera, poster paint and oil colours on cardboard which had been previously treated with a coating of size. These exercises followed lectures and practical demonstration in some particular aspect of painting, such as portrait painting. Historic examples were selected for discussion . . .'[4]

This is the tutor speaking for the benefit of art educationalists and other teachers. Tuesday nights in Ashington weren't quite like that. For a start, Lyon recognised the need to be responsive rather than bossy. In his MA thesis, written several years later, he took a more measured line, proudly admitting that, even early on, the Group had more or less determined what should be done.

'Surely, they enquired, it should be possible to gather together material for discussions on Art which will be instructive without involving the necessity either of listening to talks on Italian Madonnas or of learning how to draw and paint.' The exercises, and the Madonnas, receded. The experience became the main concern: 'to learn by "doing", and through actual working in the medium of the artist'.

'We had to consider whether it was worth while examining the methods by which a painting or a piece of sculpture was made by an artist through the process of experiencing what it felt like to make a work of Art oneself, and further, whether such an experience would help toward an understanding of Art.

'It will be obvious that without any precedent for this type of class the difficulties and dangers to our intention were formidable. Above all we had to take the risk of being attracted by technique for its own sake, and unless this temptation could be successfully avoided, our purpose

Article in *The Listener* by Robert Lyon, 1935

An Experiment in Art Appreciation

By ROBERT LYON

Mr. Lyon, who is Master of Painting and Lecturer in Fine Art at Armstrong College, Durham University, describes here the work of his W.E.A. class in the colliery town of Ashington, near Newcastle

THE elementary stages in the development of an appreciation of art are of great importance. For those who, though they have no intention of becoming practising artists, may wish to know something about the subject, several courses are available. If we ignore the man who trusts to

Lifeboat Station: painted in body colour on cardboard by Harry Young (aged 37), colliery blacksmith

his own emotions, who 'knows what he likes', there are, perhaps, two main lines of approach. One is to study the subject historically, to learn to admire, under suitable guidance, the qualities of the great masters of the past and present, to *contemplate*, and so to form a standard of values. The other approach is to learn by *doing*, to develop appreciation through an inside knowledge obtained through actual working in the materials.

The former method is perhaps the most usual, and it no doubt has its advantages. On the other hand, the training of taste by the exclusively 'contemplative' method is a long business, and the pupil must rely on the instruction of opinion outside himself—a reliance which easily produces conventionality, timidity, and even insincerity of mind. Appreciation should be developed from within. It should not be based on a series of 'reach-me-down' opinions of others.

A start, then, I believe, ought to be made from some personal experience of our own so as better to appreciate the experience, both practical and theoretical, of others. The difficulty of taking the initial step in art-appreciation was a problem with which we were concerned in the formation of a W.E.A. class in Ashington last Autumn. The members of the class consisted of

men associated directly or indirectly with the collieries of that district, having little or no previous experience in art appreciation. Ashington is a town of 30,000 inhabitants some twenty miles from Newcastle, and is entirely dependent on the collieries round which the town has grown. It is not a suburb of a larger town and it does not boast of any cultural amenities other than those which are the outcome of the formation of W.E.A. and similar classes. It has no Public Library but is served to some extent in that direction by two Workmen's Institutes. The latest of these, which has been built within the last four years, does offer some scope for the procuring of books on subjects other than fiction. The nearest available examples of historic and modern art are housed in the Laing Art Gallery, Newcastle. Yet, if the resources of the locality were of the meanest order, the spirited quality of members of the class in their interest in art was inspiring. The possibility of arranging a programme was discussed by members of the class and it was decided that we should attempt an approach to the appreciation of art through some understanding of the methods and media used in the execution of various branches of art, and that we should do it through actual experience of self-expression in those media. The programme was not in any sense of the word an adaptation of the normal course followed in a School of Art, or of that of the training of an artist, but one which, it was hoped, would provide the class with a creative experience, and would so help them to appreciate better the creative experience in others.

East Wind: tempera panel by H. P. Wilson (aged 33), dental mechanic

would be defeated. We realised at the beginning that there was a very real danger that, through handling materials, the Group might develop into an Art Class or Sketch Club for those members who had any technical skill.

'The intention of this creative "Art Experience" which was to be the basis of the class experiment was to provide the members with a "fellow-feeling" through technique for the practising artist; in other words it was intended to help them towards a better appreciation of the "Art Experience" of others, and it was by keeping to this rule throughout the first months of the experiment that the first of the principles was established, namely that EXERCISES IN TECHNIQUE WERE NOT TO BE CONSIDERED AS PICTURE MAKING IN THE PERMANENT OR EXHIBITION SENSE OF THE WORDS.'[5]

The stress Lyon placed on the throwaway nature of the exercises was partly explained by the lingering WEA strictures about learning for the sake of learning to no practical end and partly by his own attitude, his sense of his own expertise. 'It must be remembered,' he said, 'that the Ashington class has little in common with, say, a class in Art Appreciation in Golders Green or Basingstoke, Hull or Eastbourne.' He, as the trained professional, well equipped to execute portrait commissions, to paint major murals, couldn't help but be uneasy at the thought of such unprofessionals – artists from nowhere – getting ideas above and beyond their class status. Ordinary amateurs were no competition; ordinary sketch clubs were obviously incapable of ruffling professional feathers. But the Ashington miners were a breed apart; their growing enthusiasm was bound, eventually, to rule him out. No wonder therefore that, in his public statements, Robert Lyon represented the whole initiative as a form of inspired homework.

'Each week he'd give us a title and we were supposed to go away and produce a picture by the next week,' Harry Wilson said. 'Do what you like how you liked with what you liked: any sort of cardboard.'

As Oliver Kilbourn remembered it, 'Lyon said "I think we'd better start you painting so you can get some inkling of what an artist has to do to create a picture. You might learn something from your struggles." He gave us some subjects like "Dawn", "The Hermit", "Deluge". He had the religious angle in mind for that one but I did a deluge in an ordinary working street: waves coming down the street and thunder and clouds sort of faffing, but no biblical idea about it at all. So Lyon then said "I tell you what, you can have your own titles and paint your own experiences." Technique was second. Idea was the foremost thing that mattered.'

Kilbourn's *Deluge* is a small, dark catastrophe. Houses are overwhelmed by the violence of a storm generated in distant parts. It is ordinariness drowned in emotion.

Even in the first Ashington paintings artlessness gives way to

Oliver Kilbourn, *The Deluge*,
one of the first subjects set

cautious ambition. Compare *The Hermit* by Harry Youngs, a simple
arrangement of trees, hut and rain-butt in a dell and the hermit an
uncomplicated, bearded figure, with Oliver Kilbourn's *The Hermit*: a
different sort of painting, based on a real character who lived on the
beach at Lynemouth, designed to bring out the aggressiveness of a
recluse, the idea of smouldering despair.

'I haven't been one for the usual pursuits of pitmen,' Kilbourn said.
'I didn't go in for keeping whippets or pigeons or growing leeks; I
wasn't even a club man, not to any extent. I took a great desire to
express myself not with any thought of gain or anything like that but I
couldn't express myself so well in words and I found that I could
express my feelings and what I wanted to get over in drawing and
painting.'

By the sound of them, most of the subjects set by Robert Lyon – they
included 'Spring', 'Rest', 'Age and Youth' and 'Sunday Morning' –
were straight from the teachers' manual or a Patience Strong calendar.
He had no thought then of encouraging the systematic depiction of

Ashington life or of stimulating what the politically-minded took to be 'proletarian' art. Lyon's article in *The Listener* of 29 May 1935, written as an end of term report on the first series of classes, was concerned only with 'the elementary stages in the development of an appreciation of art'. Even so, the five paintings reproduced, of which two survive, reveal the emergence of a distinctive body of work.

Robert Lyon's 'An Experiment in Art Appreciation', *The Listener*, 1935

Pit Ponies, Sunday Morning, by Arthur Whinnom, who alternated with Harry Wilson as WEA branch secretary, is the sort of picture to be expected of a keen student showing willing. The ponies, a basic breed with heads in profile and pit-prop legs, are enjoying their freedom. Whinnom ('aged 33, a colliery clerk', the caption said) is 'not concerned with the technical difficulties of drawing in such a choice of subject'. Nor is Harry Youngs ('aged 37, colliery blacksmith'), whose *Lifeboat Station* is Newbiggin's answer to Alfred Wallis, with a vertical sea curtaining the right hand side. Harry Wilson's *Sunday Morning* and *East Wind* are more studied, more calculated.

East Wind became one of the Group's exemplary paintings. It was reproduced in colour in Commander Stephen King-Hall's *Mine* ('a magazine for any intelligent person of any age who has a shilling and is interested in all sides of this tremendously interesting modern world'), illustrating Wilson's account of 'An Adventure in Art' which came between pieces on 'The Green Woodpecker' and 'Guide Dogs for the Blind'. It was said to have been his first picture. In it, disposed around a street corner that presents all the essentials of two-point perspective,

George Brown, *The Poacher*, 1935

The Miner: oil painting on cardboard by Leslie Brownrigg (aged 29)

duction to the various branches of painti
and while the lack of facilities prevented ar
very elaborate practical experiment, some of
the various methods which painters used in
the past were considered and explained. Experiments were executed in tempera, poster
paint and oil colours on cardboard which
had been previously treated with a coating
of size. These exercises followed lectures
and practical demonstration in some particular aspect of painting, such as portrait painting. Historic examples were selected for
discussion of the different techniques used
in a Botticelli, a Van Dyck and a Goya. In
the demonstration the class was able to see
the work in progress, and to examine the
canvas, paints and brushes; they also gained
some actual experience of the building up of
a painting. In this way they were stimulated
to ask questions not only about the various
media but about the advantage in varying
circumstances of one medium over another.
They would ask, for instance, when tempera
might be considered a more suitable medium

The course was one of eighteen lectures or meetings, and
the procedure followed consisted of the selection of some
typical examples from various periods of painting illustrating
imaginative composition, design, portraiture, water-colour and
engraved work. These examples were analysed separately in
lecture form, and some aspect was chosen for discussion, this
being followed by a demonstration of the particular medium
used and by an exercise attempted by members of the class.
First came a discussion on engraving; historic and modern
examples of the various processes, possibilities and limitations
were examined and the tools explained. For the purpose of
reducing the principles of the engraved line to its elementary
form, experiments in linoleum cutting were attempted and
printed by the class. The selection of subject matter used for
the exercise was left to the individual student, and it was
readily appreciated by the class that the limitations of this
particular medium called for some idea which would be capable
of a simple treatment. They could appreciate, too, the restraint
imposed by the medium, and the fact that simple massing and
the use of the engraved line form the only means of expression.
This helped them to appreciate at once these artistic qualities
in the work of others. Such an understanding of the material,
its limits and its possibilities, whether it be in a woodcut, a
steel-engraving, or a book illustration, helps to increase in a
remarkable way the faculty of discrimination in pictorial art
of this nature. The same programme was followed in the intro-

Pit Ponies, Sunday Morning: painting on paper
by A. F. Whinnom (aged 33), a colliery clerk

than oil paint, why today some painters
prefer to work in one medium rather than
any other, and why one artist uses a heavy,
full paint, and another a delicate palette.
Again, during the study of examples of
imaginative composition some contact with
the creative minds of the artists was established, for the class began to understand
the control of the medium under the hand
of the artist. The idea the artist attempts to
express is presented to his mind and through
his control of the medium used.

I do not suggest that the perfect technician
is the best artist. There is such a thing as
inarticulateness, and the technician may
have nothing to express. But treatment of
the material is an essential part of art. Gains-
borough, Rubens, El Greco, Van Gogh,
might be cited as examples of artists who,
working in the same medium, responded in
quite different and individual ways to the
stimulus and suggestion of the material.

During discussion and in practical essays

Sunday Morning: another tempera panel by H. P. Wilson (aged 33)

Harry Wilson, *East Wind*, 1935

George Brown, *My Uncle*, 1935

saplings whip in the wind, figures are tugged, a newsboy blows on his fingers and, to leeward, three becalmed shoppers look at a shoe display. 'Obviously the simple record of an emotional experience,' Lyon said; but *East Wind* is more than that. It's the first of the Group's factual accounts of what everyone in Ashington felt and knew. Here, captured for good, is the impact of a wind straight off the North Sea.[6]

The Miner, by Leslie Brownrigg, also pointed the way forward from Lyon's article, introducing what was to become the Group's abiding theme: the recording of an existence as remote from notions of prettiness or high aesthetics as could be. 'The instinctive use of massive forms in a cramped space is clearly the result of a familiar experience,' Lyon commented. Leslie Brownrigg, the miner-turned-school-teacher, imposes silence. The forms are indeed massive and the effort of bending and lifting and heaving coal into a tub is made so deliberate it borders on dumb show. The painting is a sort of revelation. Paintings like this made it plain that, beyond being incompatible with the Art Appreciation classes of Eastbourne or Golders Green, the Ashington WEA class was entertaining unique possibilities.

'The early shyness at expressing themselves did not last long after they had accepted the idea that they were not making pictures for pictures' sake. They found out that they had begun to establish a real and personal contact with Art and that they as a Group were indeed talking to each other in a way that they had never done before. It was very thrilling, for me,' Lyon added, 'to watch these ideas take shape.'

During the winter of 1935 Lyon arranged for the class to go to Newcastle one Sunday morning and see the watercolours in the Laing Art Gallery. The Director, Bernard Stevenson, showed them round. That was one objective achieved: art made accessible. Also, at the end of his *Listener* article, Lyon mentioned that members of the class were planning to go on excursions into the countryside. This too encouraged him to 'believe that the scheme is capable of further development, not only in Ashington but elsewhere'. Guided tours and sketching expeditions, however, proved less important than what had already been established on Tuesday nights: not so much the contact with Art, as Lyon put it, as the growing assumption that the Group had its own strength. 'You know, I get a new sort of kick in using my hands and making things,' said Harry Wilson during a wireless broadcast a few years later. 'When I paint as we do in our Group, I have a feeling of freedom; here I find an outlet for other things than earning my living; there is a feeling of being my own boss for a change and with it comes a sense of freedom.

'When I have done a piece of painting I feel that something has happened not only to the panel or canvas, but to myself. For a time I have enjoyed a sense of mastery – of having made something real.'[7]

3

Ashington has always been the home of surprises
and we have long since ceased to marvel at anything.

RIDLEY WARHAM, Managing Director
Ashington Coal Company, 1938

A road stretches to the horizon, snow on either side and frozen spoil heaps ranged along the edge of the trench in which pipes are being laid. The night-watchman warming his hands at the brazier looks up to see the sky lighten. George Brownrigg's Walpamur on plywood *Dawn* was painted in 1937, harking back to one of the first set subjects and to the time when the Group met and worked in isolation.

'You go right the way into the picture to where the sun is rising,' Oliver Kilbourn said, echoing comments made when Brownrigg originally brought the painting to the YMCA hut for discussion. 'Somehow it seems to be miles long that road; it seems to emphasise the long night, the long wait of the watchman.'[1]

Classes resumed in the autumn of 1935 and one night Robert Lyon introduced the Group to a complete outsider, someone from the world of Modernism: Helen Sutherland, who lived about twenty miles away at Rock Hall just north of Alnwick. The first time she came Lyon went to the trouble of getting hold of a partially draped model – which meant lowered blinds – so as to impress her with the art school character of his course. Miss Sutherland arrived in a Rolls driven by her chauffeur Mills. Surprisingly, perhaps, the evening was a success. She invited them to Rock Hall for tea and to look at her collection.

Helen Sutherland's father had been chairman of P&O for more than thirty years and her mother had left her a fortune. She was a Liberal and, for a while, a Quaker, generous, possessive and frugal, eagerly acquiring – and then often giving away – whatever seized her attention. 'Rather Abbess-feeling in this Abbey-like house of Rock', she was both patron and hostess. Ben and Winifred Nicholson were friends of hers and David Jones stayed at Rock for months at a time. He repeatedly drew the view from his bedroom across the grounds to the church, which he saw as an Arthurian Chapel Perilous and for which she assumed responsibility. She had it repainted white every year and gave it a Ben Nicholson offertory box.[2]

David Jones, *The Chapel in the Park*, 1932

'Life in Ashington was very very dull in those days,' Harry Wilson said, 'so to go up there – quite a short run on the bike – was a real tonic. She invited us up quite frequently, especially if she had a new picture or pictures, and in this way we came into contact with current painters.

'We'd not experienced this sort of thing before and we certainly hadn't met a practising painter producing the abstract work that Nicholson was doing. So gradually our horizons were widening. You could really get down to it and talk about their pictures with the artist and really get to know what he was driving at, and you found that he was quite ordinary in a way, nothing to be afraid of: a person tackling a job.

'David Jones was a very quiet, retiring person, yet when you got him talking, talking about the things he was interested in, which was what he liked to talk about, he was quite interesting. He was very interested in mental pictures he had of the First World War and men working in saps and in trenches and the effect of the war and the atmosphere around them. We had many a talk about that in the garden there, walking round, but you never knew when you had him: his mind was off on another angle altogether in a second or two.

'Miss Sutherland expected you to be able to stand up and account for your activities. She would stand in front of a picture with you and ask precisely why this was done this way or why that person was included, and you couldn't put her off. She was very perceptive and very rarely did you find out how her mind was working.

'Some of the pictures were quite acceptable to anyone but I'm afraid other pictures carried a challenge for certain people. I had no particular religious feeling or anything like that and Miss Sutherland was very definite about that sort of thing, so I never got beyond talking about pictures and aesthetic-value-of-pictures. The content, the social content, we didn't talk about.'

Oliver Kilbourn too found it difficult to discuss his mining pictures with her. 'It was rather against her grain to think that men were working in such conditions as that, you know. The gulf didn't seem to matter when we were in her presence though. She always made us at ease and actually during tea she was much more a woman concerned with dishing out the tea: that was another side to her. But when it came to pictures it was very definitely another side.' She was particularly proud of her Mondrian: *Composition, White and Red*, 1935. 'She didn't like pictures really that had a lot of colour. She liked pictures that were more or less greyish.'

'We used to take a few pictures, maybe,' Jimmy Floyd added. 'We'd look through them and she would say if she liked this one or that. We took twelve one time, and when we got back home she wrote to Arthur Whinnom, who was Secretary then, saying now I would like to buy George Blessed's picture and Mr Floyd's picture. Arthur came down to see me and I said "Arthur, *give* her my picture. I can always paint another picture, but," I says, "we could never get another Miss Sutherland."'[3]

Thanks to Helen Sutherland the whole class – all twenty-four plus Robert Lyon – went to London for a weekend, at her expense, primarily to see the great Royal Academy Winter Exhibition of Chinese art. It was for all of them apart from George Brown, who had worked down there years before as a joiner, their first visit to London. Indeed, for several it was their first time south of the Tyne.

Arthur Whinnom distributed a cyclostyled itinerary listing studios, galleries, a housing estate and the BBC, and later, soon after they returned, wrote a long and ecstatic account of the trip, parts of which were published in the *Morpeth Herald*, toned down a little for the wider readership.[4]

Arthur Whinnom, *Sea Coal*, 1936

They met under the clock in Newcastle Central Station at 10.15 pm on Friday, 14 February 1936. 'The roll was called – scarcely necessary perhaps – because nothing short of an earthquake in the vicinity of Ashington would have prevented that appointment being observed.'

Kenneth Clark had reviewed part of the Chinese exhibition a month before in *The Listener*. He sounded a touch bored.

'A limitation may often be a source of strength or at least of perfection, and no doubt Chinese painting owes some of its perfection to the fact that it does not attempt to go outside a narrow range of colour and seldom tries to express any emotion other than a contemplative detachment. Our distracted painters may sometimes envy the tranquillity – I might even say the resignation – with which generations of Chinese artists sat down to paint a misty river or two sparrows on a twig. And yet we feel that an art so limited can never achieve universal greatness.'[5]

Jimmy Floyd, *Flowers*, *c.*1935

Harry Youngs, *The Hermit*, c.1935

Oliver Kilbourn, *The Hermit*, c.1935

Andy Rankin, *In the Canteen, c.*1935

Leslie Brownrigg,
The Miner, 1935

George Brownrigg, *Dawn*, 1937

Oliver Kilbourn, *Duke Street 2 am*, c.1937

Harry Wilson, *10 am*, 1937

Harry Wilson, *Ashington Colliery*, c.1936

Oliver Kilbourn,
Saturday Night, 1936

Harry Wilson,
*Roundabouts and
Swings*, 1937

Andy Foreman, *The Bar: Playing Dominoes*, c.1936

Oliver Kilbourn, *The Dogs*, 1936

William Scott, *The Bedlington Terrier*, 1937

Arthur Whinnom couldn't have disagreed more. 'What is to be said about this overwhelming concentration of the personal expression, in beauty of form and colour, over sixteen centuries of time, of a people of famed cultural attainment . . . there is an affinity between the people who created those studies we looked upon, and ourselves; there is nothing suggesting a tortuous mentality, but rather, a lofty, poetic, yet simple expression of the sublimity of nature and the beneficence of religion . . .'

'The Tate Gallery was our next adventure – there Mr Ede met us and, after lunch, conducted us to some people we had long wanted to meet, Cézanne, Van Gogh, Sargent, Seurat, Manet, Utrillo. Mr Ede gave us many valuable pointers in the way to approach these individualists – we studied and absorbed and were well content. We also saw some of the moderns, David Jones, Kit Wood, Ben and Winifred Nicholson – all of these were particularly interesting to us and a happy renewal of acquaintanceship.'

Outside the Tate there was a pea-souper, which Oliver Kilbourn later painted from memory, the backs of buses blurring into the pervasive grey.

Their hired bus took them to Edward Halliday's studio in Barons Court. Then 'On. On ye braves! – Mr Halliday accompanying us, we descended upon Mr Alfred Hardiman, St John's Wood. Never shall we forget the sight that greeted us as we thronged into his spacious studio, Cathedral-like in its loftiness. Occupying the centre and heart of it was his Haig Equestrian, a magnificent and noble tribute to a great soldier

Oliver Kilbourn, *London Fog*, 1936

Harry Wilson, *Convalescent*, 1936

and gentleman. It rose in soft whiteness, a harmony of shapely majesty, fourteen feet high from the base on which it stood. We were fortunate in getting this preview as it was ready for the foundry to be cast in bronze.' (Hardiman's statue was destined for Whitehall.)

'We were a snowball party by this time, and we swept up Mr Hardiman and proceeded to the BBC and the music-hall programme. Ten of the party were permitted to attend the actual broadcast – the remainder were accommodated in one of the listening rooms of the new BBC building. We distributed ourselves in comfy chairs and lounges in a softly-lit and sound-proof room and settled down to hear radio such as the proud set owner never dreamed possible – free from banshee wailings and the related tribe of "noises off". Will Fyfe and his brother and sister entertainers set the seal on a perfect day

Hotel. – Oblivion   Breakfast. – Ready!

Sunday 16th February
(Bound for Lark Hall Rise Estate)

'On the way, Mr Austin Child chatted on Architecture – his examples to hand as it were – as we took advantage of the better visibility and thronged the top deck of our bus.

'Lark Hall Rise is something more than a housing scheme, it is an achievement of housing vision. Numberless flats and maisonettes are included in stately buildings – college like in their sense of spaciousness and peace. Quadrangles and gardens. Many aids to housewifely comfort such as hot water from central boiler – (the plant attended by a porter attached to each block) – laundries and drying rooms at the top

of the building – a gardener to keep trim the lawns and flower beds . . .
Mr Soissons planned it and succeeded in housing four times the
number of people on the ground space formerly occupied by the
ordinary two-storey house.'

Hampton Court was next, and then the National Gallery. 'Mr
Robert Lyon was our information bureau and we kept him busy. Many
of the pictures were familiar to us of course, in print form, but the
enjoyment of the original far transcends the pleasure of seeing a good
print.'

Cream tea, with madrigals to follow, was provided by Mr and Mrs
Ede in their seventeenth-century Hampstead house, the first version of
what was to become a celebrated exercise in applied tastefulness: Jim
Ede's Kettle's Yard Gallery in Cambridge, filled with Ben Nicholsons,
Christopher Woods, choice pebbles and Gaudier-Brzeskas for the
edification of undergraduates. 'Tea,' Arthur Whinnom told the *Morpeth Herald*, 'was taken in a candle-lit room, with the grey fog shrouding
everything outside.'

'Homeward bound – thudity-thud, powerfully potent, – dead logs all
through the night, – early morning, Newcastle, and back to the grind –
Monday's!

'However, "Begone dull care!" . . . we have sojourned for a while in
a goodly land and have walked under the palm trees and the acacia
groves and have companioned with people of our own mind and our
souls wax strong within us.'

A.F. WHINNOM

The London weekend, with its mixture of Lyon and Sutherland
interests and connections, was doubly important to the Group. Oliver
Kilbourn remembered, above everything, the art.

'To me it was a terrific experience. The Chinese art: I hadn't seen
anything like it. The thing that impressed me most was *The Flight of the
Hundred Geese*, it was a long scroll about thirty feet long, from the
source down to the sea and you walked along, kept walking down and
reading the scroll as you went, and that seemed to me to be something
like the idea of Hogarth and Bewick: sort of an additive painting rather
than looking at just one picture. You went along with the thing.'[6]

Forty years later, in his sequence of paintings 'My Life as a Pitman',
Kilbourn went back to that long, horizontal, narrative scheme.

Harry Wilson reckoned the 'Art Pilgrimage to London' (as the *Morpeth
Herald* headlined it) changed the WEA class's idea of itself. 'The
most important thing probably about it was that we began to feel like
a unit, a group of people that had somewhere to go, something to do,
some real important work to do. When we got back we were offered one
or two opportunities for exhibition and it became almost a duty then
to find something to do to justify the interest that had been taken in us.'

ART FROM ASHINGTON

Students interested in the work of the Ashington Art Appreciation Group, on exhibition at the Hatton Gallery, Armstrong College, Newcastle.

Art Experiment at
Ashington Tri...

Art Appreciation

By their exhibition of paintings and engravings, opened by Sir William Marris in the Hatton Gallery of Armstrong College last night, the members of Ashington Art Appreciation Group are making a little history and at the same time courageously demonstrating their faith in the purpose of the Group. The exhibition should attract considerable attention, especially from other colliery areas. It tends, for one thing, to dissipate that fatal self-consciousness that smothers the desire in many people for self-expression in art craft forms, and the feeling for a more intimate awareness of the significance of light and colour, line and plane in the production of beauty. Apart from its educational value, such study as this Group has undertaken should provide stimulating contacts and recreational content during the processes of seeking to arrive at a true appreciation of art as expressed by the masters.

NORTH MAIL 16.C

CATALOGUE OF AN EXHIBITION OF PAINTINGS
BY MEMBERS OF AN ART APPRECIATION GROUP,
ASHINGTON, NORTHUMBERLAND

HATTON GALLERY
ARMSTRONG COLLEGE
NEWCASTLE UPON TYNE

NOVEMBER 16th to 21st, 1936
OPEN FROM 10 a.m. till 9·0 p.m.
SATURDAY 10 a.m. TILL 1 p.m.

4

*The revolutionary coal-miner conceives no better
life than that of the reactionary owner.*

CLIVE BELL *Civilization*, 1928

The Ashington Group's first exhibition was held in the Hatton Gallery, Armstrong College, in November 1936. Opening it, Sir William Marris the College Principal said, 'I think this exhibition must be one of the most remarkable displays that have been shown in this gallery,' adding that 'the choice of Ashington as a site for this class seems to me to have been a very gallant one.'

His was the tone of one used to offering congratulations at degree ceremonies. 'There are some very sympathetic renderings of tired men enjoying their rest and relaxation after toil. There are beautiful harmonies of colour and some bold reachings after harmony in design. There is spontaneity and there is naturalness. Surely some of these unsophisticated paintings remind us of modern work?'

The ninety-seven paintings shown, together with a number of engravings, were taken to be specimens of progress. 'Art Experiment At Ashington Triumphs' said the *North Mail* and Robert Lyon, in his catalogue introduction, emphasised the rapidity of advance.

'Some of us who had the honour and pleasure of accompanying this group to the Chinese Exhibition and to the Tate Gallery can testify that the insight into painting which this experience of painting itself has begun to breed is nothing less than astonishing.' A photograph in the *North Mail* showed appreciative young women students gazing at pictures close-hung in a corner of the gallery. One, either George Brownrigg's *Spring* or Harry Youngs' *Sheep Farm* or Ed Hedley's *Sheep*, impossible to tell which – can be made out clearly enough to explain why the three students (probably trainee art teachers) were so enthused. They were seeing the new teaching methods pioneered by Marion Richardson extended to adults, unlikely adults at that.

By the mid Thirties Marion Richardson was the most renowned art educationalist in Britain. As a London County Council Inspector of Schools and as a lecturer everywhere from Lambeth to Vancouver she propagated her belief, developed in the first place at Dudley High

School, that teachers should 'abandon the formal syllabus of work which hitherto had guided them and trust to the children's natural interests to be the mainspring of their art teaching.' Herbert Read, reviewing her 'Writing and Writing Patterns' in *The Listener* less than a month after the appearance of Robert Lyon's article on his WEA class, remarked that 'every kind of evidence – anthropological, psychological and experimental – tends to show that what Miss Richardson rightly calls the creative activity in children is "native" and "inborn", and must be educated (that is to say, brought out) and not imposed by the dulled and impotent sensibilities of adults.'[1]

Having abandoned Art Appreciation in the usual evening class sense, and having avoided anything approaching art school instruction, Robert Lyon was presenting 'creative activity' of a novel kind. He described the exhibition as 'an external sign or symbol of the principle of "seeing by doing"', adding, as if to cover his tracks and head off his colleagues, that the principle was of course a matter 'of learning to appreciate and to enter into the heritage of painting by working in the material of painting itself'.[2]

Harry Youngs, *Dawn*, 1936

Lyon selected the 1936 exhibition. It was very much as he wanted it: the model for others to be inspired by, possibly to emulate, and the basis for a thesis. Lyon favoured the naïve. The three paintings he chose to keep for himself, *Flowers* by Jimmy Floyd, Harry Youngs' *Dawn* (a black cock crowing in a Cheviot landscape) and Harry Wilson's *East Wind* were to be his lasting reminders of the success of an extra-mural commitment he had taken on for idealistic reasons and, incidentally, to supplement his salary. They were charming. They were no threat to his own hard-won professionalism. *Flowers* and *Dawn* especially suited a certain kind of Thirties decor.

Hand-blocked curtaining, shelves of yellowy French paperbacks, a *Vertical Form* or somesuch by Moore or Hepworth on the mantelpiece, an unplastered chimneybreast painted white, with a sparse Ben Nicholson in a Bourlet frame: this was Herbert Read's study in the Mall Studios, Hampstead circa 1936. To the Left, in terms of outlook, with Finmar furniture and stark picture windows, was what Osbert Lancaster labelled 'Functional': the habitat of the modular intellectual. To the Right, Chelsea way, was the pickled white-on-white of Syrie Maugham interior design. A Floyd or a Youngs would have appeared perfectly fitting in such rooms, fresh and potent and interchangeable with an Alfred Wallis, say, or an Utrillo or even a Cedric Morris or a Christopher Wood. Children's art, folk art, the 'primitive' in diverse forms were regarded as desirable foils to sophistication. They reinforced notions of progressiveness through 'anthropological, psychological and experimental' liberating approaches. The artless Youngs or Floyd was bound to gladden the eye of any Modernist out to redefine beauty and rediscover innocence.

In his introduction to Marion Richardson's *Art and the Child*, published in 1948, Kenneth Clark wrote that 'she always discouraged the feeble fantasies, the shallow day-dream pictures into which children so easily subside. She saw to it that all their images should be taken from the life they knew, and she was able to do this because she herself could see beauty in the "little shops, market stalls, chimney-stacks, watchmen's huts, eating houses, slag heaps, canal barges, pit mounds, and waste ground".'[3]

Such subjects – the stuff of Ashington Group painting – were unlikely to please those who had no choice but to put up with difficult circumstances and mean surroundings year in year out. 'Many pictures would be thrown away because of lack of space in small houses,' said Oliver Kilbourn's wife Peggy. 'Mining pictures would not be welcomed by wives to hang on walls at home; landscapes would be considered more suitable. The women had enough of mining dominating their lives and frequently, when there were several workers in the house, reducing them to slaves. Many of the women were never able to go to bed except at weekends and just dozed in a chair to fit in with the different shifts.'[4]

Van Gogh had come to recognise that 'to express hope by some star, the eagerness of a soul by a sunset radiance', would do more for the mining communities of the Borinage than any number of grim pictorial exposés. The version of the *Sunflowers* in the Tate was the seventh of Newnes' *Modern Masterpieces* (a shilling-a-fortnight partwork published in 1936, to which Oliver Kilbourn subscribed), sandwiched between Sickert's *Ennui* and *Ballet Girl and Dressmaker* by Laura Knight. Van Gogh, Frank Rutter stressed in his note on the picture, 'had the courage to see commonplace things, not in a commonplace way, but with an eye dilated by poetic imagination'. This, rather than the cultivation of naïvety, was the proper aim of the Ashington painters once past the stage of introducing themselves to themselves. 'It sounds rather crude,' Van Gogh wrote, 'but it is perfectly true that the feeling for reality is more important than the feeling for pictures.' By the time he came to write his second catalogue introduction for his 'University Tutorial Class, Ashington WEA', Lyon was echoing Van Gogh: 'To learn to see familiar objects with fresh eyes . . . surely this is an enlargement of spirit which makes, at least in one direction, for better and happier human beings? It is no escape from reality; rather it is a readjustment to reality . . .'[5]

Harry Wilson's *Ashington Colliery*, an oil painting from 1936 (probably *Pits*, number 88 in the Hatton catalogue), is an example of the transformation of artlessness into painstaking knowledgeability. Unlike the others, who hadn't been much affected in their painting by seeing works by modern masters in London, Wilson was patently impressed by Cézanne. The roofs and siding could be from the

environs of Aix; the pit heap is a man-made Montagne Sainte-Victoire. The painting is precisely composed and laid down; chimneys, winding gear, wasteground and huts are given geometric functions beneath a busy sky where smoke fades into white.

Ashington Colliery is a scene dignified by art. Oliver Kilbourn's *Evening Paper*, on the other hand, and his *Progging the Mat* are affectionate accounts of domestic life, the handling gentle, the observation deft. Kilbourn was already venturing beyond the charmed world of the primitive or naïf into the complexities and risks of art that isn't made simple to please.

A photograph taken in 1938 by another artist, Julian Trevelyan, come to see them at work in the YMCA hut, shows the leading members bunching up, pencils poised, self-conscious. There is no embarrassment though: drawing appears a natural activity, as straight-forward and as sociable as rag rug making, as everyday as reading the newspaper. In the foreground Harry Youngs pauses, abstracted. Oliver Kilbourn, standing next to George Rowe, who is seated on the left, has a proper drawing board with clips holding the paper. Harry Wilson, in

Photograph of the Group at work by Julian Trevelyan, 1938. Left to right: G. Rowe, O. Kilbourn, H. Wilson, A. Rankin, A. Whinnom, H. Youngs (foreground), G. Brownrigg, J. Floyd, G. Brown, A. Foreman, unidentified, L. Brownrigg

Harry Wilson, *Committee Meeting*, 1937

front of the cupboard marked 'WEA' where unfinished pictures were kept, sports an oil painter's palette. Andy Rankin is behind him, half-hidden; Arthur Whinnom is at the head of the table, his paintbox resting on some mugs; the rest, all seated, are George Brownrigg, Jimmy Floyd, George Brown with the specs, and Leslie Brownrigg. There is an air of confident absorption.

The other end of the old army hut appears in Harry Wilson's *Committee Meeting* which shows members of the WEA branch committee sitting around the stove discussing matters. The painting, as described by Wilson to the compère Leslie Mitchell on television in November 1938: 'There was only one light and that was very dim. Old Mr Knox was in the chair to keep us all in order. I was always amused by the very comfortable position Mr Watson took up, half-facing the Chairman,' Wilson was supposed to say (though, in the event, they abandoned the script). Years later, commenting on the circle of serious faces, he remarked: 'One thing about Ashington: there's very little snobbish class distinction. You can make an error or a mess of things and still be accepted as a reasonable person.'[6]

South of Ashington and outside the coalfields, the image of miners and mining communities still largely derived from D. H. Lawrence ('strange isolated dignity . . . as if a hard, horny shell enclosed them all,' he wrote in *The Rainbow*); from melodramatic sources such as the best-seller of 1935, A. J. Cronin's *The Stars Look Down*, set in County Durham ('Snow has to fall at moments of great calamity, and it duly falls');[7] from passing strangers like J. B. Priestley in his *English Journey* of 1934 ('Who wants to know anything about miners, except when an explosion kills or entombs a few of them and they become news?'); from photographs of deplorable housing and of unemployed Welsh miners singing for pennies in Piccadilly. As Priestley said, 'Pitmen are not familiar figures in the streets of our large cities.'[8] One reason why the Ashington WEA class found such a welcome in London from sculptors, curators and the BBC was that they were assumed to be sons of toil, straight from the bowels of the earth (actually only Oliver Kilbourn and Jimmy Floyd, at that time, worked constantly underground), and they came as envoys, so to speak, from a nether culture.

Someone who didn't meet them was Clive Bell, whose firm belief it was that a miner was a 'Bill Jones' sort of chap, incapable of higher aspirations than those stimulated by greed and envy. 'The revolutionary coal-miner conceives no better life than that of the reactionary coal-owner,' he boomed from his Bloomsbury perch in *Civilization*: 'rum and milk before breakfast, and breakfast of four courses, a day spent in pursuing and killing, or in some bloodless pastime, champagne at dinner, and long cigars after, an evening at the movies or music-hall, with an occasional reading of Miss Corelli and Michael Arlen, *The Mirror*, *John Bull* or *The Strand Magazine*, and all the time a firm theoretical belief in the sanctity of the marriage-tie and a genuine detestation of foreigners, artists and high-brows. That is a life that would suit Bill Jones just as well as it suits Lord Maidenhead.'[9]

The South began to throw out feelers towards miners, (almost synonymous, for these purposes, with the unemployed) as worthies, *pace* Clive Bell, to be cultivated. In the December 1935 issue of the WEA's *The Highway*, immediately after Robert Lyon's 'Approach to Art' article, and opposite a reproduction of a watercolour of two trees by Robert Buckingham (Police Constable) who was to win a place in literary footnotes as the friend of E. M. Forster, Stanley Casson reported on 'Another Approach to Art'.

'An experiment has recently been attempted at the Russell-Cotes gallery at Bournemouth, with most interesting results. The lecturer showed a series of lantern slides, without comment, to a group of unemployed. The audience was then asked to vote on the pictures shown, and the result showed "a remarkable coincidence with the opinion of the people who profess to know", which suggests (as I have always believed) that the "man in the street", if not bullied by critics,

PELICAN BOOKS

A 1 THE INTELLIGENT WOMAN'S GUIDE (1)   Bernard Sh
A 2 THE INTELLIGENT WOMAN'S GUIDE (2)   Bernard Sh
A 3 LAST AND FIRST MEN   Olaf Staple
A 4 DIGGING UP THE PAST ★   Sir Leonard Wool
A 5 A SHORT HISTORY OF THE WORLD ★   H. G. We
A 6 PRACTICAL ECONOMICS
A 7 ESSAYS IN POPULAR SCIENCE ★   G. D. H. C
A 8 THE FLOATING REPUBLIC   Julian Hu
A 9 A HISTORY OF THE ENGLISH PEOPLE (1)   Dobrée and Manwar
A 10 THE MYSTERIOUS UNIVERSE ★   Élie Hal
A 11 THE GREAT VICTORIANS   Sir James Je
A 12 THE INEQUALITY OF MAN   various auth
A 13 LIBERTY IN THE MODERN STATE   J. B. S. Halda
A 14 SOCIAL LIFE IN THE INSECT WORLD ★   Harold J. La
A 15 THE GROWTH OF CIVILISATION   J. H. Fab
A 16 A HISTORY OF THE ENGLISH PEOPLE (2)   W. J. Pe
A 17 A BOOK OF ENGLISH POETRY   Élie Hal
A 18 AFTER THE DELUGE   ed. G. B. Harri
A 19 MEDIEVAL PEOPLE ★   Leonard Wo
A 20 VISION AND DESIGN   Eileen Pow
A 21 AN OUTLINE OF THE UNIVERSE (1) ★   Roger
A 22 AN OUTLINE OF THE UNIVERSE (2) ★   J. G. Crowth
A 23 RELIGION & THE RISE OF CAPITALISM   J. G. Crowth
A 24 PSYCHOPATHOLOGY OF EVERYDAY LIFE   R. H. Tawn
A 25 ONLY YESTERDAY (1) ★   Sigmund Fre
A 26 ONLY YESTERDAY (2) ★   Frederick Lewis Al
A 27 UR OF THE CHALDEES ★   Frederick Lewis Al
A 28 CIVILIZATION   Sir Leonard Wo
A 29 LIMITATIONS OF SCIENCE   Clive B
A 30 A HISTORY OF THE ENGLISH PEOPLE (3)   J. W. N. Sulliv
A 31 MY APPRENTICESHIP (1)   Élie Hal
A 32 MY APPRENTICESHIP (2)   Beatrice We
A 33 TOTEM AND TABOO   Beatrice We
A 34 SCIENCE AND THE MODERN WORLD   Sigmund Fre
A 35 THE GREAT VICTORIANS (2)   A. N. Whiteh
A 36 THE COMMON READER   various auth
A 37 SOCIALISM IN EVOLUTION   Virginia Wo
A 38 ART IN ENGLAND ★   G. D. H. C
A 39 THE CENTURY'S POETRY 1837–1937 (1)   ed. R. S. Lamb
A 40 THE CENTURY'S POETRY 1837–1937 (2)   ed. D. Kilham Robe
     ed. D. Kilham Robe

★ Illustrated

PENGUIN BOOKS LTD., HARMONDSWORTH, MIDDLESE

Complete list of all Penguin Books at end of this volume

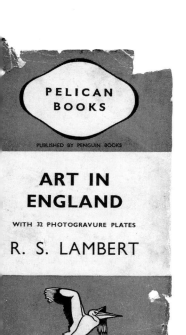

has a very fair idea of what is well done and what is badly done in art.'[10]

On similar lines, but using original paintings, the British Institute of Adult Education held some exploratory 'Art for the People' exhibitions in the Spring of 1935 in three test areas: Swindon, Silver End in Essex, where Crittall windows were manufactured, and Barnsley in Yorkshire, chosen because it was a mining district.

Reactions were positive, according to W. E. Williams who set up the scheme. 'We have at each exhibition people we call observers. They really are spies and eavesdroppers in a friendly way. If they hear a blunt Yorkshireman say to his wife as he turns abruptly away from a picture: "Well, that's not *my* idea of a cherry tree" – or whatever it is – it is the observer's job to barge in, in a casual way, and start an argument. It *isn't* his job to contradict – you don't enlighten anyone that way.'[11]

Most people, observers reported, preferred 'pictures that look real'. Williams concluded his article optimistically. 'In some places it has led people to start art clubs where, by trying to paint or draw themselves, they do at least discover how rigorous the practice of an art is.'

In October 1938 Pelican Books – very much the WEA in paperback – brought out *Art in England*, edited by R. S. Lambert, a selection of pieces that had appeared in *The Listener* (of which Lambert was Editor) during a period when, to make up for the wireless being all music and words, it gave special emphasis to the visual arts. There were essays by Clive Bell and Kenneth Clark; Moore on Sculpture, Coldstream on Painting, Stanley Casson on A. F. Hardiman's controversial Haig statue and Herbert Read twice: on 'Why the English Have No Taste' and on 'Teaching Art to Children', his eulogy of Marion Richardson which went in Section V: Art and Education, together with 'Art for the People' by W. E. Williams and, to 'show that some progress at any rate is being made in the direction of bringing (opportunities) to working people in the North of England', Robert Lyon's 'An Experiment in Art Appreciation'. With William Scott's *Bedlington Terrier* reproduced in photogravure between a splashy picture of the Cup Final by John Hiller (aged 7) and Hardiman's Haig memorial, photographed *in situ* in a deserted Whitehall, Lyon's account of 'Seeing by Doing' now looked like a manifesto.[12]

Ashington Collieries Magazine

VOL. XVII.
No. 10.

PRICE——3d.
OCT., 1937

International & Industrial Peace.

5

*What the artist of today needs for his inspiration
is some great social driving force, a new spiritual value.*

ANDY FOREMAN 'Whither Art?',
Ashington Collieries Magazine,
December 1937

Over the weekend of 5 to 7 December, 1936, the Group's Hatton Gallery exhibition was put on show in the YMCA Hall. The *Morpeth Herald* thought this 'somewhat incongruous in Philistine Ashington', and indeed there was little positive reaction.

Harry Wilson remembered being thoroughly discomforted. 'This fellow I knew in Ashington, I'd put him in the front of a picture to show how miners get a certain crabbed shape by working underground, which in those days a lot of them did. And I was standing looking at the picture when some people came up and roared with laughter at this stupid figure of mine. Well, damn it, I'd been serious about putting this character in, and to hear people laughing at it made me think I'd done the same as them in the past with other people. So ever since that I've tried to get to know first of all what the artist is trying to *say*.'[1]

The *Ashington Collieries Magazine* became a platform for the Group. Published monthly by the Welfare Department of the Ashington Coal Company, filled with fixture lists, health and safety tips, gardening notes, 'Kiddies' Korner', 'The World of Women', jokes, 'Coming Pictures that are Worth While' at the Pavilion, Wallaw and Buffalo cinemas, the magazine was a screed of exhortations. For twopence a week, 'Take the Good Things Which Life Has to Offer You. Join the Play-The-Game Society'.

Thirteen articles by members of the Group, plus Robert Lyon, appeared between December 1936 and January 1938. Lyon wrote about 'Tradition in Art'; Leslie Brownrigg covered Leonardo da Vinci's triple genius as painter-sculptor-engineer; Edwin Harrison discussed 'Beauty in the Trivial Round' ('to the serious searcher there is a mine of wealth, well-nigh inexhaustible which will lead out into wider fields of artistic discovery'); George Brown covered 'Art Through the Ages' with particular emphasis on the prehistoric. 'The history of art in its early stages,' he wrote, 'is the history of civilization.'[2]

'To understand modern art one must trace its growth from its first stages,' Oliver Kilbourn maintained. 'The earliest artists began by representing their surroundings in the form of pictures. True, they worked very crudely in early times, but as civilization progressed art became much more complex.'[3]

The class tried sculpture. 'I remember visiting the studio of one of our foremost English sculptors,' Harry Wilson wrote in his article on the subject. 'He was creating a monument to a famous British General. The General was mounted upon a magnificent charger. A powerful beast it was in the artist's first clay model. In fact, too powerful. The great General looked quite puny by comparison. Not satisfied that the dignity which he had in mind had yet been expressed the sculptor worked upon that clay until finally, after much effort, he was able to transfer the vitality of the powerful horse to the figure of the rider.'[4]

Robert Lyon described in his thesis how Andy Rankin took to carving. 'He has, as a rule, a "little thing I'm doing" tucked away in his pocket; just as I knew soldiers to do with lumps of chalk during the Battle of the Somme.' A twelve-inch torso by Rankin was whittled from 'a piece of oak which had been part of a discarded "skid" used in the pits to trap runaway trucks from crashing. Rankin, who is a colliery clerk, in his spare time worked on this piece of wood with a sharp pocket knife removing the bruised and damaged parts until the remaining surfaces, as he said, gave him an idea . . . It was smoothed off with the aid of razor blades and emery paper, until Rankin was instinctively satisfied with the feel and shape of his carving. It lacks perhaps the true sculptural quality in that there is no feeling of depth of form; but there is expressed, apart from anything else, an unmistakeable affection for the colour, texture and attractive appearance of the oak.'[5]

In *Strain* and *Toil* Oliver Kilbourn blocked in the sense of pulling and delving, using bits of pit prop. His was a strictly formal approach, whereas Jimmy Floyd, ever the storyteller, made figures that could have fitted into his pictures: his *Deputy*, for example. 'Now this man's supposed to be testing for gas: he was made out of a hardwood chuck, a bit of beech. He's got his knee pads on and his strong boots, his battery for his lamp and the cable that runs over his head for his cap lamp.'

Some of these carvings were exhibited in the Laing Art Gallery in 1938. The most impressive sculpture produced in the Group, however, was by Harry Wilson, a few years later, by which time he had stopped being a dental mechanic. He had been used to taking casts in plaster. *Pulling Cable* is one of several sculptures designed to illustrate working methods underground. 'It's a heavy cable, about two and a half inches diameter, feeding into the cutting machine. The thing to notice about it is that there are two different points at which stress is taken by the miner. The whole idea was to show the effort the man makes working under these conditions in seams two foot to three foot high.'

Harry Wilson sculptures,
Pulling Cable (plaster) and
Laying a Pan (lead)

Another piece, equally powerful, and this time cast in lead, is *Laying the Pan*. 'This person is lifting this metal crate which was part of a conveyer which shuffled coal down the face. He's lifting this heavy pan into position: again the idea is the terrific weight on top of him and very little room to work in.'[6]

In his 'Sculpture' article in the *Ashington Collieries Magazine*, Harry Wilson mentioned Barbara Hepworth, quoting her stated desire 'to make exactly the right relation of masses, a living thing in stone, to *express my awareness and thought of these things*'. 'Clearly,' he added, 'when we know this sculptor's aim, we will not expect her to give us a horse, scenting with exquisitely carved nostrils the air. Nor will we expect some pictorial representation of Malcolm Campbell's monster car, crashing across sandy space. But instead Barbara Hepworth would, as she puts it, express her awareness and thought of these things.'

'The English are a people of watertight compartments. They do not connect,' observed G. J. Renier, author of *The English Are They Human?*, in an article for *The Studio*, November 1934, on 'The English Attitude Towards Art'. To discuss A. F. Hardiman and Barbara Hepworth, equally approvingly, within the space of a few paragraphs, was unusual in art writing at the time; Harry Wilson's article was, in a way, unique. Yet the month he published it, in April 1937, an unprecedented coming-together of artists took place in London: the First British Artists' Congress, organised by the Artists' International Association as an anti-Fascist gesture. An exhibition was held, and the Ashington Group sent some pictures. The place for them was in the 'Working Men's Groups' section on the third floor of a Grosvenor Square mansion; the Abstract section, which included Legers, Nicholsons and Moholy-Nagys, was on the ground floor; Surrealism, still fashionable, had the ballroom. There were paintings by Dali, Picasso and Magritte.

'The most cheerful aspect of this huge exhibition is its politics for they are of the Millennium,' the *New Statesman* remarked. 'The Sage Picasso hangs demurely beside the work of a twelve year old girl . . . and Mr Duncan Grant's *Policeman* is clearly neither a bully nor an *agent provocateur*.'[7] Gwen Raverat, in *Time & Tide*, said 'It is a good show from end to end' and quoted the catalogue at some length: '"The Artists International Association does not stand for uniformity of expression, for the dragooning of artists or the sinking of individuality. On the contrary the exhibition demonstrates the richness and the variety that can be produced by the vanguard."'[8] This was, declared Anthony Blunt in *The Spectator*, 'the most important event of the year from the point of view of English Art.'[9]

The Artists' International had been founded in 1933 on the return from Russia of Clifford Rowe, full of the Socialist Realism of the first

LEFT George Brownrigg, *The Kitchen*, 1937
BOTTOM Oliver Kilbourn, *Proggin' the Mat*, c.1938
BELOW Oliver Kilbourn, *Evening Paper*, 1936

Oliver Kilbourn, *Doctor Bruce*, 1936

Arthur Whinnom, *Pit Incident*,
c.1936

Harry Wilson, *House Drain*, 1938

George Brownrigg, *Shifting*, c.1937

Oliver Kilbourn, *Pithead Baths*, 1939

Oliver Kilbourn,
Bait Time, 1937

Arthur Whinnom,
Pay Day, c.1940

George Blessed, *Fish Wife*, c.1938

Harry Wilson, *Fish Sale*, 1938

Oliver Kilbourn,
Mother and Child,
*c.*1939

Five Year Plan. Artists, Stalin said, were 'engineers of the human soul' and in Britain, as in the USSR, these engineers were to work for the furtherance of Party and proletariat. The first AI exhibition, held in a Charlotte Street shop in the Autumn of 1934, was 'The Social Scene'. Eric Gill, Henry Moore, Paul Nash and the like associated themselves with the venture for the sake of radicalism and in support of the Peace Movement and anti-Fascism. Even then, the most forceful artists involved were those who mostly worked in advertising and other forms of commercial art, notably James Fitton and James Boswell, both of whom enlivened *Left Review* with their Grosz-style caricatures.[10]

By 1936 the International had widened its appeal to become the International Association and the AIA served as an artists' Popular Front, promoting Aid for Spain, shifting a little in its peace aims (Guernica was bombed the Monday after the weekend Congress) and attempting, with more goodwill sometimes than sense, to democratise the arts without the eagerness-to-instruct of the 'Art for the People' scheme.

George Brownrigg's *The Garden*, a picture of an open door with raking going on beyond, was exhibited in Grosvenor Square and used as an illustration, along with a Robert Buhler, a Moholy-Nagy and a Magritte of a sort of mirage bridge, for Herbert Read's article on the Congress in *The Listener*. Read noted that Working Men's Groups weren't producing the agitprop that some would have hoped, surely, to see. 'It looks as though the worker, in his spare time, preferred to cultivate his garden.' But then, as George Brownrigg himself had emphasised in his essay on 'Our Interest in Art' for the *Ashington Collieries Magazine*, 'Modern Art is a record of the present day,' and a picture of someone tending his plot fully deserved its place in the AIA 'vanguard' provided it was 'an impression of personal feeling'. It was a matter of regarding painting as more than a mere hobby. Boxed, like a motto, in the centre of Brownrigg's article was a quotation from Ruskin:

> Art, properly so-called, is no recreation.
> It cannot be learned in spare moments, nor
> pursued when we have nothing better to do.

The Ashington Group's alignment with Southern radicalism cannot be said to have affected it. 'Were they disturbed in the sense that such publicity affected their painting? Not a bit of it,' said Robert Lyon. 'All they asked was that the spectator should understand the conditions under which these pictures were painted.'

They weren't in the position of ex-miners turned professional artists, like George Bissill from Nottinghamshire or Vincent Evans from South Wales, for whom mining pictures were part of a repertoire based on increasingly distanced experience. Vincent Evans' paintings

'Dickie Green', by Robert Buhler

'The Garden' by George Brownrigg, from one of the Working
Men's Groups

'Le Pont d'Heraclite', by René Magritte, in the Surrealist Section

tended to be well-lit and heroic; George Bissill's underground workings were corridors as neat as de Chirico arcades where lumpy miners handled cubist boulders. Ashington Group pictures remained technically unpolished. 'You write something down, as you write a letter and leave it uncorrected,' one of them said to Janet Adam Smith when she went to see their second Newcastle exhibition, held at the Laing Art Gallery in March 1938.

Janet Adam Smith had been Arts Editor on *The Listener* before moving to Newcastle where her husband, the poet Michael Roberts, taught at the Royal Grammar School. Her successor on *The Listener*, Joe Ackerley, asked her to write an article on the Ashington Group, now more than a WEA success story, and this she did. Her account of the way they worked, and what they aimed for, gives a clear impression of their originality and independence.[11]

'They paint on three-ply or on the cardboard of Gold Flake packing cases, with Walpamur; which is easily handled and can be used as a watercolour.'

She was struck by George Brown's 'remarkable carving of *The Hod Carrier*' and by his argument that 'a miner who uses his eyes does not need any life-class or lessons in anatomy to tell him where the stress comes on a man's back and thighs when he is carrying a four-stone weight on his shoulder.'

She discussed *The Bedlington Terrier* with William Scott who painted it: his only 'Ashington Group' picture, a signboard almost, boldly red and green. 'Miners are keen on Bedlingtons, so the terrier must be painted in a mining village. The Ashington pit was put in the background; on the left was a row of miners' cottages with the Institute, and behind them was an old tower he had once seen, with pigeons. The manager's house must have a garden, and gardener; and Mr Scott wanted to set Bedlington Cross in the middle of his picture but he hadn't time to do this before the exhibition. It took him just under a fortnight to paint.'

'This picture sums up Mr Scott, I think,' Harry Wilson said in his scripted conversation for television's 'Picture Page' a few months later. 'Few of us knew very much about old Mr Scott except that he was a retired master shifter, seventy-five years old. We felt we knew something about him when we had seen his picture. There is nothing borrowed in that picture.'[12]

'Different men give different reasons for enjoying their painting,' Janet Adam Smith continued. 'One says that you make friends that way; when you are looking at a man's picture you have plenty to say to him. Another finds painting an escape from the squalor of his surroundings (but he is an exception; most of them find the suburbs of Newcastle more dreary than Ashington). He painted a village street, and says that it wasn't until he had finished that he realised how every

incident in the picture had to do with dirt–women shaking mats, cleaning boots and emptying ash-pans, a child playing in the gutter, a man shovelling coal. He knows the dirt of the place gets on his nerves; painting has brought this irritation to the surface and relieved it.'[13]

That painting, Harry Wilson's *10 am*, acquired by Bernard Collingwood Stevenson for the Laing, is North Seaton laid open: the whole place, from colliery row to colliery, pit heap, railway bridge over the Wansbeck, open sea beyond. It's more complicated than *East Wind*, more bird's-eye, more synoptic. The activities appear unconnected, each preoccupation a separate chore. Where, in George Brown's *Poacher at Dawn*, say, or Jimmy Floyd's *Winter*, the subject is treated summarily (P for Poacher, as it were, W for Winter), in *10 am* and in Oliver Kilbourn's *Sunday Dinner* (also in the Laing exhibition) there is a sense of annals in the making through the accumulation of detail.

A year or so later Harry Wilson painted *The Drain*, again showing North Seaton, this time with the intention of showing what conditions were like until a sewage system was laid on shortly before the war.

'This central drain running up the picture is the only drainage of these houses. The buildings on the left hand side of the picture contain the earth closets: this was the only drainage or sewage system for these rows of cottages. The drain was cleared out every morning by a big tap being turned on at the top of the row and each woman successively coming out and using a hard yard broom to clear her section of the drain.'[14]

Oliver Kilbourn, *Football,*
*c.*1937

The Drain is one of several paintings that deals with the sort of subject the photographer Edith Tudor-Hart of the Workers' Photo League came to Ashington to document.[15] Another is Oliver Kilbourn's *Portrait of Doctor Bruce*, though there is nothing particularly disturbing about it at first glance. The Doctor is absent; the painting shows his surgery, with file cards, dispensary, First Aid notes on the blackboard. Around the margins, in vignettes, his bicycle is seen, winter and summer, day and night, all weathers, as he goes on his calls. Whereas the Colliery doctor was paid by the Coal Company and would be expected to make light of illnesses and injuries so as to save on sick payments or compensation, Doctor Bruce was the ideal GP, conscientious, keen to prevent illness, resourceful when accidents occurred. In 1935 there were five cases of typhoid in Ashington.[16] In 1938, 858 miners, or more than one percent of those working in Britain, were killed and 131,776, about a sixth of the total, were injured and disabled for more than three days. Ashington was no worse than other mining districts; in fact, in many respects circumstances and working conditions were relatively good. When members of the Group put into pictures some of their resentments, they weren't so much propagandising as reminding one another of what they knew to be true.

'All the men insist that their work is a special affair, done to please themselves,' Janet Adam Smith wrote. 'They are shy of outsiders seeing it and criticising it as they would criticise the work of full-time artists. They don't want to become full-time painters. They don't want to send in work to the Royal Academy or the London Group. They

Photographs of Ashington
Colliery by Edwin Smith,
August 1936

don't want to be looked on as curiosities, publicised by dealers as
"Miner Painters" and made a collectors' fashion. Their only motive in
selling their pictures (at a pound or thirty shillings) is to get money for
painting materials and their only reason for exhibiting them now is to
stimulate other tutorial classes to try the same experiment.'

The possibility of other groups forming, on the principles of seeing-
by-doing and, as Arthur Whinnom said, producing pictures that 'were
not pictures in the accepted sense of the word but were essays in the use
of materials,' was repeatedly raised both by Robert Lyon and by others
with special interest in the spread of either 'workers' art' or self-
improvement. Unemployed clubs, art clubs attached to Health Centres
or arts centres such as the Bensham Grove Settlement in Gateshead
looked to Ashington for inspiration, found it but failed. Usually the
reason was that, instead of treating painting as an unartistic exercise,
tutors and students fell for sketch club and life-class routines. Elsewhere, it seems, there was never the strength of purpose. 'A big factor is
not resenting criticism,' Harry Wilson said. By 1938 the Ashington
Group was becoming aware that it was unlike any other, that organisations like the AIA or the British Institute of Adult Education had
greater need of them, as a phenomenon, than they had of any outsiders.
It was at this point that they became subjects and objects of Mass
Observation.

6

*A person with a public school background can understand
the ideas and attitudes of a cannibal Malekulan as
easily as he can understand those of a Welsh coal-miner
or a Bessarabian.*

TOM HARRISSON *Savage Civilisation*, 1937

Having read Janet Adam Smith's article in *The Listener*, Tom Harrisson immediately wrote to Robert Lyon and they arranged to meet in Newcastle.[1] Harrisson was excited: the Ashington Group sounded just the job, a ready-made unit of working-men painters, 'unprofessional' painters as he put it, painters working 'without one eye on the collector and the other on Jan Gordon'.[2]

Harrisson was an enthusiast. 'Life was an ascending fantasy,' he wrote in *Savage Civilisation*, a book about his experiences – and the European experience – in the New Hebrides, where he had gone with an Oxford University expedition in 1933. He had stayed on, going native to some extent, and had left Malekula in November 1935 aboard a yacht belonging to 'a little swarthy fellow' who turned out to be Douglas Fairbanks Senior. *Savage Civilisation*, richly strewn with cannibalism, sexology and oral history, was one of the most successful Left Book Club publications of 1937. By then Harrisson had turned his attention to a sort of anthropology nearer home.

'The wishes and needs of mankind are rendered accessible, on a class-basis, to the artist-scientist, but the nature of his field of inquiry, as scientist, or his subject-matter, as artist, is found to extend beyond himself as observer,' wrote Charles Madge in *Left Review* in February 1937, adding, 'his observations must be mass-observations, his data mass-data. His works of art must satisfy not his own isolated fantasy but the needs and wishes of the masses; his scientific generalisations must apply not only to himself but to every member of his society.'

Madge, a poet turned *Daily Mirror* journalist, had sociological leanings. He and Harrisson, together with the poet, painter, film-maker Humphrey Jennings, set up Mass Observation in January 1937 as an encyclopaedic cross-cultural exercise, designed to achieve a redistribution of knowledge. Henceforth the 'masses', the unheard

Still from *Coalface*, documentary film directed by Alberto Cavalcanti and edited by William Coldstream

voices of that overwhelming proportion of the population who never featured in the gossip columns, were to be systematically sounded out and studied in every aspect. Nothing was to be too trivial to note and tabulate: audience behaviour, mantelpiece ornamentation, pub codes, courting procedures, dirty jokes, funeral practices, quack medicaments, attitudes to authority. Madge the poet and Harrisson the anthropologist exchanged roles. Madge eventually became a professor of sociology while Tom Harrisson made demands on his teams of Mass Observers that escalated from the mundane to the ridiculous to the surrealistic.

Mass Observation procedures were essentially a matter of taking notes and keeping files, but at an early stage in his Bolton (or 'Worktown' as he called it) project, a concerted investigation of the Lancashire way of life, Harrisson summoned artists to do fieldwork for the cause. William Coldstream and Graham Bell came and painted views of backstreets and mill chimneys from the roof of Bolton Art Gallery; Michael Wickham and Julian Trevelyan, more venturesome, went into the streets, where Trevelyan made reportage collages, using torn up *Weekly Illustrateds* and the like. Harrisson sent the artists round the pubs soliciting comments on such works.[3]

A number of Mass Observers were working class, many of them would-be writers who came forward in response to the publicity, but undeniably the whole enterprise depended on public school educated stalwarts: the leftish intelligentsia. The Ashington Group were ideally qualified, it seemed to Harrisson, to serve as MO's North Eastern cell: on the spot, motivated and, above all, authentic.

Julian Trevelyan, as a member of the great Northumberland family that included Sir Charles Trevelyan and G. M. Trevelyan, had regional credentials; so he accompanied Tom Harrisson to Ashington in September 1938. Harrisson was fresh from giving a talk, for Guy Burgess, on the BBC about 'Art and the Working Chap' (meaning 'What They Think in Worktown'), so he was keen to make this a recruiting drive. They stayed with George Brown and his wife for a week. According to Robert Lyon's son Peter, Lyon wasn't told and resented Harrisson's intrusion. 'Most important of all,' Harrisson advised the reader in *Living Among Cannibals* (his child's version of *Savage Civilisation*), 'when one goes to live among primitive people . . . one should observe their customs and manners and do the right thing.'[4] That, he assumed, meant taking crates of beer for the chaps. But most of them didn't drink; and while Trevelyan paid ten shillings a day for his board, Harrisson left at the end of the week without bothering to settle up. George Brown, irascible at the best of times, was furious.

They came with preconceptions of life in a pit village: Lawrentian conceptions of the 'primitive'; Orwellian images of hard graft (*The Road to Wigan Pier* was another Left Book Club choice in 1937); the gritty fervour of Auden's 'lurcher-loving collier black as night' from the GPO documentary *Coal Face* of 1935 edited by William Coldstream. They had little idea of the spirit of the Group. Trevelyan sketched, seeing motifs at every turn, and he took photographs with his Leica of the Group, summoned to demonstrate what one of their working sessions was like. Tom Harrisson described the set-up.

'To paint in, they have had the occasional evening use of a hut in a backwaste behind the Buffalo Cinema.

'There may often be singing of hymns and psalms from the tiny fundamentalist gospel hall on the one hand, while boys play riotous games in the room on the other side. For this, half a crown a time, two naked electric light bulbs, two rough tables and hard wood chairs. On these they sit, with wood or paper balanced on knees, smoking, talking, whistling, everyone painting straight out of the mind, without preliminary sketches or looking at things, yet often with such accuracy and intimacy that one can scarcely credit it. It is one of the oddest sights, a little dilapidated room full of men in working clothes, all sitting round

Photograph by Julian
Trevelyan of the Group. Left
to right: Kilbourn, Youngs,
Whinnom, Brown.

Julian Trevelyan, drawing of
Ashington, 1938

The Committee and Members of Bensham Grove Settlement, Gateshead
and the Members of the Ashington Art Group

cordially invite you to attend

AN EXHIBITION OF PAINTINGS
BY UNPROFESSIONAL PAINTERS

A Collection of Work brought together from various parts of
England; to be held at

THE SETTLEMENT from OCTOBER 8TH to the 22ND,

and to be Opened

On SATURDAY, OCTOBER 8TH, 1938

at 3·30 p.m., by

Michael Roberts

(Author of "A Critique of Poetry" "The Modern Mind" etc.)

CHAIRMAN : VICTOR CLARK
Assistant Director of Education for Northumberland.

R.S.V.P. [P.T.O.

In connection with the Exhibition a series of
lectures will be given at the Settlement at 8 p.m.
on the following dates, on the subject of :—

"Vision and Social Realism."

Thursday, October 13th. TOM HARRISON
(Director of Mass Observation).
"SOCIAL REALISM: WHAT DO WE MEAN?"
Friday, October 14th. SERGE CHERMAYEFF,
F.R.I.B.A.
(Architect of the B.B.C. Studios and
other important modern buildings).
"ARCHITECTURE AND EVERYDAY LIFE."
Monday, October 17th. MICHAEL SPENDER,
F.R.G.S.
(Expert on Aerial Photography and
Survey. Twice a member of Mt.
Everest Expeditions).
"VISION AND THE REALISM OF OTHER
CIVILISATIONS."
Tuesday, October 18th. CHARLES MADGE
(Poet—c.f. "Oxford Book of Modern
Verse" etc., and Editor of "Mass
Observation").
"POETRY AND EVERYDAY LIFE."
The Public cordially welcomed to the Lectures.
No charge for Admission.

A special Week-end Session for Discussions on
"Painting and Realism" will be held on October
15th—16th. Chairman: WILLIAM HICKEY (of The
Daily Express).

For full information, apply to the Warden, Bensham
Grove Settlement. Phone : 72263.

turning out these pictures without any effort, even any apparent thought'.[5]

Had he thought, Tom Harrisson would have realised that 'working clothes' were not worn. Trevelyan's photographs show this to have been very much a collar-and-tie occasion. But then Harrisson was writing from the viewpoint of one who had spent time in all manner of exclusive places: 'A club house: this is the place where the men talk unwomanly things, where they gather to plan in the evenings, talking out daylight . . . All men and clubs are part of the village; that is the wider coherence. The club is a smaller, more frequent loyalty . . .'[6] Harrisson in a Matanavat longhouse, learning about 'pig-pride' and other Malekulan cultural factors, is the same Harrisson, four years later, coming to quick conclusion about Ashington.

The Ashington Group was not signed up as a Mass Observation unit; however, there emerged from the week the idea of a weekend of staged discussions together with an exhibition of 'Unprofessional Painting'. This was arranged for October at the Bensham Grove Educational Settlement in Gateshead.

'Very busy indeed,' was J. B. Priestley's comment on the Settlement, having visited it in the course of his *English Journey*.[7] It was a detached house with a small theatre in the garden and other annexes, a 'Good Works Settlement', Julian Trevelyan called it, where WEA classes

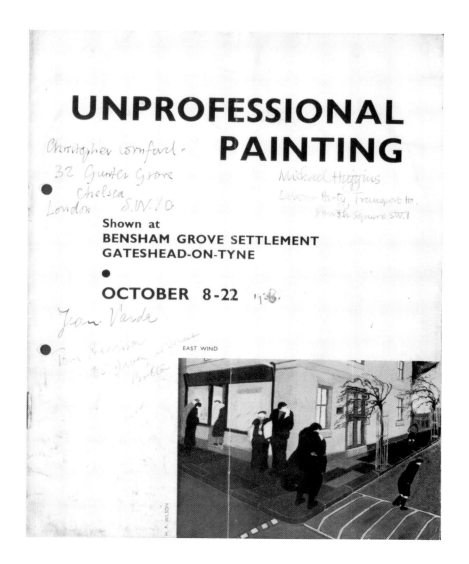

UNPROFESSIONAL PAINTING

Christopher Cornford.
32 Gunter Grove
Chelsea
London S.W.10

Michael Higgins
Labour Party, Transport Ho.
Smith Square SW.1

Shown at
**BENSHAM GROVE SETTLEMENT
GATESHEAD-ON-TYNE**

OCTOBER 8-22 1938.

Jean Varda

EAST WIND

H. P. WILSON

were held (including an 'Appreciation of Art' series run by Mrs D. M. Lall from the University) and a whole range of activities, from drama and embroidery to the Girls' Life Brigade.

The exhibition was to be held from 8 to 22 October and to include, besides thirty or so Ashington paintings, groups of works by self-taught or 'outsider' artists. Lucy Wertheim of the Wertheim Gallery in Burlington Gardens was to lend a number of paintings by Alfred Wallis, by Vivin, the retired French postman, by Henry Stockley the Green Line busdriver, and by David Burton the pavement artist. Trevelyan, Roland Penrose, Bryan Guinness and others lent some of their discoveries and the Haslemere WEA Art Class, comprising two Post Office clerks, a housewife, a wool shop proprietor, a ship's steward and a farm labourer, were to send drawings.

In the event, fifty paintings by the Ashington Group were shown, plus a dozen or so sculptures. The paintings from Mrs Wertheim's gallery were priced at ten guineas (for a Wallis) to fifty guineas for a Vivin: professional prices. The Ashington paintings were £2: a week's wage.

Because the whole occasion was intended to prove a Mass Observation point and, indeed, to be another round in an artworldly critical debate centering on definitions of Realism and on the politics of Realism versus the politics of Abstraction, the publicity was important. Tom Driberg ('William Hickey') was asked to chair the debate on 'Painting and Realism', later changed to 'Anyone Can Paint'. Allen Lane of Penguin Books was invited, and Sir Kenneth Clark, but he couldn't come, the Warden of Bensham Grove told Arthur Whinnom, 'although he would have liked to very much, and is very interested in the Exhibition'.[8]

James R. Spencer, of the Newcastle *Sunday Sun*, a columnist who listed 'birds, Christianity, my health and the art of the working man' as his main interests outside the family, was approached by 'Julian, nephew of Sir Charles Trevelyan, and famed Surrealist painter'. As a result, apart from a few inches on Amy Johnson, Spencer's entire 'Northern Pageant' column on 25 September, a day of headlines about Hitler's Sudetenland ultimatum, was devoted to Mass Observation and the Ashington Group. He quoted at length from an essay written by Harrisson for the 'Unprofessional Painting' catalogue, using his description of the Group at work, dropped from the catalogue presumably because someone noticed that it could be regarded as condescending; besides Harrisson, as usual, ran on a bit. Spencer took the opportunity of recommending some of his favourite working men artists: 'Mr Oswald Bage, the Durham miner who has founded the Consett Art Club and also the work of the six men, three of them miners, who constitute the art class of the Spennymoor Unemployed Settlement under the capable leadership of Mr W. G. Farrell'.[9]

Harrisson was determined to put across his belief that 'from the Ashington Group (so far the only group), as from the isolated working class individuals painting often in almost exactly the same way in America, on the Riviera, in Paris, London, Newcastle, Cornwall and South Wales, we get a consistent common denominator, an LCM, as it were, of expression in paint. For in all these pictures there is one unmistakeable quality – simplicity, but simplicity which is natural, and which has something to say.'[10] In other words, where the MO slogan was 'They Speak for Themselves', here was 'They See for Themselves'.

Harrisson then spun a theory about lack of perspective being an essential, a simplistic view which he turned into a swipe at Coldstreamism. 'The greater part of art teaching consists in learning perspective and balance, ideas much prized by professors, but also by moderns, like the well-meaning Social Realist School, strongly left-wing in politics, declared revolutionary, who paint portraits of rich women, Charlotte Street cafés, and Sussex landscapes, while they run a strict art school in the Euston Road.' Perspective, Harrisson implied, is anti-life. 'To the ordinary eye, things are largely "flat".' The ordinary being, to his mind, valuable in itself, it followed that anything else was pretentious.[11] One gets the impression that Harrisson was hoping to achieve in Gateshead, with the *News Chronicle* and the *Daily Express* in attendance, a more famous debate than the 'Realism-Surrealism' set-to organised by the AIA at the Group Theatre six months before, when Jennings, Penrose and Trevelyan opposed Bell, Coldstream and Peter Peri the concrete sculptor. On that occasion, according to the Surrealists, they won. This time, with the focus shifted, the Unprofessional was tipped to win.

Elaborate preparations were made. The exhibition was to be opened by Michael Roberts and lectures were to be given the following week by Harrisson ('Social Realism; What do we mean?'); by Serge Chermayeff (co-architect of the Bexhill Pavilion, a cultural centre for the South

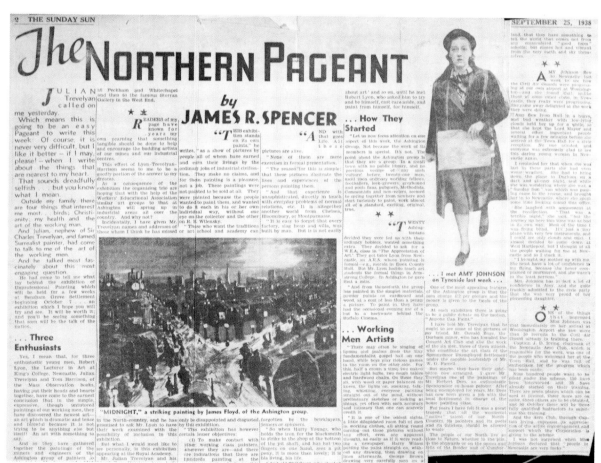

Coast) on 'Architecture and Everyday Life'; by Michael Spender on 'Vision and the Realism of other Civilisations' and by Charles Madge on 'Poetry and Everyday Life'. D. R. O. Thomas, warden of Bensham Grove, wrote to Arthur Whinnom suggesting tea after the opening and weekend accommodation at the Settlement on a self-catering basis, apart from Saturday tea and Sunday lunch. 'The international tensions of last week looked like upsetting arrangements,' he added, but despite the Munich crisis he hoped that there would be a good turnout from London, as well as the eleven from Ashington. 'I think it will be that most of them will be putting up at the Settlement in the same way as yourselves, so you should have a jolly time!'[12]

In his autobiography, *Indigo Days*, Julian Trevelyan recalled that 'we most of us slept on camp-beds in the classrooms above the exhibition, and it was noticeable that the Ashington miners all produced the most elegant striped silk pyjamas, while Tom, Michael Wickham, Varda and myself had only a few rags, if anything at all to sleep in. We sang "Ilkla Moor" and other songs till late at night.'[13]

Memories of the weekend are confused, not only of the type of pyjamas worn, but also of the programme followed. Michael Wickham had an idea that painting classes for all concerned were held in Ashington. That was unlikely, as no one else remembered anything of the sort. Humphrey Spender however took photographs of the Group of work in the YMCA hut – probably during the previous week – and a

Tom Harrisson speaking in the Bensham Grove Settlement debate, photographed by Julian Trevelyan, October 1938

few more shots survive of the Mass Observers, seven abreast, striding through what looks like Byker in Newcastle, and enjoying the view from the Tyne Bridge. Julian Trevelyan had a vivid recollection of the Group and the visiting team sitting in a pub listening to Jean Varda, the Greek artist, telling 'one of his interminable fantastic stories: mermaids and sea nymphs wafted message to porpoises in submarine green temples of sapphire and coral . . . the Ashington Miners were spell-bound.'

A photograph by Trevelyan in the Mass Observation archive is the best evidence of the style of debate. Tom Harrisson, in an open-necked shirt, is speaking, probably about social perspective or essential simplicity. His audience, mostly wearing jackets and ties, is attentive. Paintings are hung haphazardly and propped on the mantelpiece of what was once a dining room by the look of it. They include Harry Youngs' *The Gardener* and George Brownrigg's *Kitchen*. No one is paying attention to them, for this is Tom Harrisson's moment.

Tom Driberg, sitting next to Tom Harrisson, reported on the proceedings in his William Hickey column the following Tuesday.

'A number of professional artists, intelligentsiacs etc went up from London mostly to speak against it ('That anyone can paint').

'It sounds an absurd statement, too baldly put. Opposition chipped away at its wording. Yet it withstood chipping . . .

Mass Observers on Tyneside, photographed by Humphrey Spender, 1938

'Apart from the miner-painters themselves – only one of their group, a teacher, spoke against the motion – it was supported by *Julian Trevelyan*, wild-haired, lanky ex-surrealist in whose Hammersmith studio you may see such objects as a corset riding a bicycle; by Mass Observation's *Tom Harrisson*; by Greek-born mosaicist *Jean Varda*.

'Speakers against included *Geoffrey Gorer* who has written successful books about Africa, New York, the Himalayas and *George Downs*, who sells women's underwear in the Caledonian Market: his opposition was telling for he has some pictures in the Gateshead show, has been trying to paint for years, said he knew he still couldn't.

'I disagreed.

'The motion was carried.

'I liked the North.'[14]

The *Northern Echo* had given more details the day before.

'George Brownrigg said "The thing was to go in and have a try". He contended that the success of the Ashington Group was typical of what anyone could do.

'Mr Geoffrey Gorer the traveller and art critic opposed the assertion and said he could not paint although he had tried.

'Julian Trevelyan believed that the Ashington Group was part of a movement which would make painting as common an art as music once was in this country. Professional painters need have no jealousy: the greater interest that was taken in painting the more interest there would be in their own work if it was worth it.

'He also believed that increasing leisure was inevitable and painting by everybody was one of the ways of usefully employing such leisure.

'Arthur Whinnom, colliery clerk and secretary of the Ashington Group, claimed that people had hereditary gifts which made it possible for them to paint but that the art was latent in everybody.

'George Downs: "There must be certain conditions in which the disease breaks out."

'Robert Lyon summed up: "Painting offers the simplest technique of self-expression. It was unlike the piano or the flute which required a special technique."

'The motion was passed by a vote of about 40 to 20.'[15]

The weekend was deemed a success. To the Group it had been a wonderful chance to meet other sorts of artists. They had felt awkward, most of them, and they had wondered at times what the whole thing was in aid of; but looking back it was a turning point: the end of the beginning of their venture. 'To meet on common ground the brilliant young artists of today, men of keen mind and wide vision, is a valuable experience for working men,' the *Morpeth Herald* commented the Friday after. 'I hope, all the same', the writer added, 'that our artists will not become over-exhibited, or that they will ever allow themselves to be exhibits themselves.'

Certainly that was a possibility. While the Ashington delegation went home and resumed work, the 'intelligentsiacs' went off to Jesmond to be entertained by Janet and Michael Roberts and to Corbridge, to stay a night with Robert and Mabel Lyon. A tour was planned, to the Pioneer Health Centre in Peckham, to Fulham Public Library, the Wertheim Gallery and Mansfield Art Gallery. Broadcasts were to be arranged (also coinciding with the publication of the Pelican *Art in England*) and, wildly optimistic, Julian Trevelyan declared, 'It is my belief that there is no town or community where it would not be possible to form a group somewhat on the same lines and achieve very much the same results.'[16]

This didn't happen though. For one thing, Mass Observation, in the person of Tom Harrisson, moved on to other preoccupations. 'Can Science answer the question of a woman's charm?' he demanded in the *Sunday Graphic* on 30 October. 'It is doubtful. But the researches of Mass Observation have. Not good at telephoning. Not good at . . .', and he was away. The Ashington Group played no further part in MO. The interest aroused by the showings in Peckham, Fulham and Burlington Gardens was muddled somewhat by the presence of so many other 'primitive' paintings alongside the selection from Ashington. A 'mass picture' was attempted at the Private View, with Tom Driberg contributing the first stroke, followed by David Burton the lionised pavement artist. 'By the time I left,' the *News Chronicle* reporter wrote, 'the rather Bloomsbury private viewers had made it look like any decent picture at any decent private view. I wonder what the unprofessional painters will make of it?'[17]

Tuesday NEWS CHRONICLE November 8, 1938

Northumberland Miners' Paintings On Show

Among the 150 " unprofessional paintings " in an exhibition which opens in London today are several by Northumberland working men. The two pictured here are (left) " Dawn," by James Floyd, and (right) "The Committee Meeting," by Harry Wilson—both Ashington miners. Another picture on Back Page.

Such stunts were hardly in the spirit of 'seeing by doing'. The Peckham Health Centre, privately developed, in a new, airy Owen Williams building, was designed for families in a limited catchment area with a nursery, clinics, reading room, swimming pool, café, dance-floor: every facility for well-being. An Art Group must have seemed an obvious, and easily arranged, additional attraction. Yet nothing happened. It was all too utopian; besides, those who took an interest in the exhibition often got it wrong. Jill Adam, in the *News Chronicle* 'Leisure Corner', used it as a cue for exhortation: 'I am told that the wives of the Ashington Group are very chary of putting their husbands' colourful work in the parlour. Well, now, come on women, we can't let the menfolk get ahead of us with art in the home. After all, that *is* our province.'[18]

On 8 November Mary Adam wrote to Robert Lyon making final arrangements for an Ashington Group item on 'Picture Page' from Alexandra Palace. She thought the script he had sent was 'just a little too highbrow. Wilson might well have written about the "fabric of the mind" but I don't think he would say it.' In the event, the script was scrapped and Lyon and Wilson both appeared in the afternoon edition, and Wilson only in the evening, talking to Leslie Mitchell. Harry Wilson, who had been issued with a lower class railway ticket for the journey South than Robert Lyon, thought the whole BBC exercise showed a 'certain "other-rank" attitude.' It was partly the tone of the two versions of the script, in which Leslie Mitchell was made to spell out the difference between Lyon and his chaps. There was reference to the 'decorative panel' he had just completed for the Essex County Hall: a work in a highly professional tradition. The Group, by contrast, was cast as chorus, not unlike those who sang in the streets: heroic in their despair.[19]

Assumptions were easily made. The *News Chronicle*, for example, couldn't quite understand why the Ashington paintings in Peckham showed so few signs of bitterness or reproach. There had to be an explanation: after all, statistics and documentaries told a different story. If these painters weren't liars then they had to be escapists. 'They are romantic, for the most part, these miners, reflecting little of the realism of gloom, courage and struggle which is to be seen among the pit-workers of Northumberland.'

On 17 November 1938 Robert Lyon wrote to Oliver Kilbourn asking a special favour.

'Dear Mr Kilbourn,
Would it be at all possible for you to come in to the college on Saturday morning and to bring your pit clothes with you so that I can do a really good drawing? If this is possible I will pick you up in Ashington and we could make a day of it . . .'

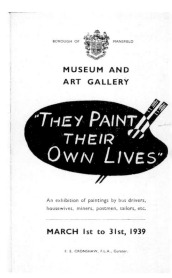

BOROUGH OF MANSFIELD

MUSEUM AND
ART GALLERY

"THEY PAINT
THEIR
OWN LIVES"

An exhibition of paintings by bus drivers,
housewives, miners, postmen, sailors, etc.

MARCH 1st to 31st, 1939

F. E. CRONSHAW, F.L.A., Curator.

Drawings of Oliver Kilbourn
by Robert Lyon, 1938

Lyon's drawing of the head of Oliver Kilbourn is heroic in the Eric Kennington idiom: the miner as front line combatant. The drawing is accomplished; it would have served well as a detail in some great mural scheme commemorating underground valour. When it was done it represented a sort of conclusion to a year in which the romantic notion of miner-painters threatened to mask the reality of Tuesday nights in the YMCA hut. 'In notoriety,' the *Morpeth Herald* reminded the Group, 'there lurks danger.'[20]

7

*As things are, spare time is a time when we have a chance
to do what we like, a chance to be most ourselves.*

HUMPHREY JENNINGS *Spare Time*, 1939

TOP Still from Humphrey
Jennings' film *Spare Time*,
1939

BOTTOM Still from Carol
Reed's film *The Stars Look
Down*, 1939

Those going on shift enter the cage and hold themselves rigid for the
drop. With Laurie Lee's comfortable voice rounding off the commen-
tary, Humphrey Jennings ends the eighteen minutes of high teas,
cinema, amusement arcades, band practice, allotments, whippets and
dance he called *Spare Time*. The film was made in 1939 and, even by
GPO Film Unit standards, it was hardly a box-office success. Unlike
Carol Reed's 1939 screen version of *The Stars Look Down*, for MGM,
which was applauded for its combination of documentary-style realism
and elemental passion.

'This is the story of simple working people . . . simple working
people', it begins, the voice-over intoning across the pithead and pit
rows of a supposedly Tyneside ('Tynecastle') mining district. Michael
Redgrave plays Davie Fenwick, the studious lad who suffers at the
hands of the no-good Emlyn Williams and a grasping Margaret
Lockwood, his personal setbacks eclipsed in the end by a pit disaster.

The Stars Look Down was conceived as a serious social drama, a
Geordie *Germinal*, and it coincided not only with *Spare Time* but also
with the coming-of-age of British photo-journalism in *Picture Post*.
Some of the establishing shots of back-alleys come close to Harry
Wilson's North Seaton; there's the same scattered activity, the same
range of bystanders. In *Spare Time*, on the other hand, Humphrey
Jennings strings complete vignettes together, contrasting kitchen and
rehearsal room, a cycling excursion and doing the pools, late-night
window shopping and street games. This is Mass Observation entering
into the mood and waxing poetic. The most poignant and surreal
moment comes when the girls of the Manchester Victorians' Carnival
Band tramp across a fogbound football pitch, kazoos bleating, jaunti-
ness fading as a tatty processional effigy of Britannia is manhandled
into view.[1]

When Jennings ran *Spare Time* for his Film Unit colleagues the
reaction was sniffy. Basil Wright said, 'He seemed to show, in our

[87]

Still from *Spare Time*, 1939

opinion, a patronizing, almost sneering attitude towards the efforts of the lower-income groups to entertain themselves.' This was the usual complaint about Mass Observation; that 'I the Camera', so to speak, assumed the right to go poking into everyone's affairs. In retrospect Wright changed his mind. *Spare Time*, so redolent of Mass Observation in its Worktown phase, now appears more humane, more responsive and infinitely more imaginative than the average cinematic paean to the British Worker ('British Workers', incidentally, was its working title). *Spare Time* was in its way a homage to the Unprofessionals.

While Mass Observation's pooling of enthusiasms and date gave the generally pious and banal output of the Thirties documentarians fresh grounds and a whiff of surreality, the dictates of MO photography gave the *Daily Mirror*'s 'Lensman', Humphrey Spender, endless tasks. He followed funerals in Bolton, loitered in Blackpool funfairs, braved the hostility of pub regulars, stood outside mill gates during the evening rush concealing his camera as best he could, hoping he wouldn't be noticed. Spender's 'Worktown' photographs often look like stills anticipating characteristic Jennings sequences. Less formal than Bill Brandt or, rather, less inclined to retouch dramatically or exaggerate by darkroom means the blackness of Depression in County Durham,

TOP Photograph of the Group by Humphrey Spender, 1938

BOTTOM Photograph by Humphrey Spender of the allotments at Ashington, Woodhorn Pit behind

Spender nonetheless experienced the same compunction as Brandt. The diffident photographer, always on the threshold of other people's worlds, feeling intrusive, couldn't hope to match the friends-and-neighbours informality of, say, Oliver Kilbourn's *Saturday Night at the Club*.

The first issue of *Picture Post*, published on 1 October 1938, immediately set a new tone in reportage. Besides being less cluttered than *Weekly Illustrated*, more sure of itself, *Picture Post* had the clear idea that the interest of a documentary is essentially narrative. Hogarth, 'himself a man of the people, wanted to paint people as he really saw them', it said and, besides featuring Hogarth as an exemplar, the magazine had a Hogarthian look at 'The History of the Corset' and 'The Men who Built the "Queen Elizabeth"'. In the second week there was greater confidence; 'London by Night', 'Spinsters' and 'And Again: Back to School' set the *Picture Post* style. In the twelfth week an article by Michael Roberts on Tyneside appeared, giving a view that brought a protest from the Lord Mayor.[2]

'Geordie,' Roberts wrote, 'looks after his whippet or his pigeons, he goes to the dog-races, fills in his Pools coupons, lets the Missus have her fortune told by the Stars, and behaves like a quiet, decent citizen even in the worst of times.' The text was brief, almost irrelevant. The captions were stiff with facts ('In Gateshead 28.9 per cent of insured workers were unemployed in October this year. In South Shields it was 31.2 per cent . . .'); but the pictures were eloquent. Humphrey Spender had spent a week taking them and had also been to Ashington, as a Mass Observer paying his respects. The Group welcomed him and Oliver Kilbourn showed him round. Like Edwin Smith, who had photographed Ashington Colliery in August 1936, Spender seemed particularly struck by the back-of-beyond situation of Britain's largest pit village. He went to the allotments, his Surrealist's eye fancying the bedsteads used as pergolas, his MO eye noticing the territorial aspect, the sense of male preserve, his Lensman's eye drawn to the pigeon crees, with their castellations and bold paintwork, and the pigeons themselves, fluttering free.

Jimmy Floyd's *Pigeon Crees*, with Woodhorn Colliery in the background, is Spender's location from a different perspective. To Spender the place was strange and fascinating; to Floyd it was homely, a happy, self-contained world. It would be wrong, obviously, to imagine that Jimmy Floyd was anything but a naïve in his approach to art. As he said, 'I don't think I've been influenced by anybody. I just sit down and paint what I want to paint to suit myself.' But in Oliver Kilbourn's drawings of 'A Boy's Day', done around this time, there is a narrative scheme worthy of *Picture Post*. By going back twenty-five years or so he went beyond photo-journalistic bounds, conscious that he could search his memory for 'the picture that nobody has painted before'.

Newcastle: Evening On The New Bridge

Twilight is kind to Newcastle. The bold lines of the New Bridge stand out sharp against the sky. The lights in factories and offices show bright against the gathering light. All that is commonplace or mean fades out of sight.

TYNESIDE

A Picture Post cameraman spent a week in Tyneside. He saw grand, but gloomy, views. He saw some poor architecture, but splendid engineering. He saw some prosperity. But he saw much more poverty. He saw the irrepressible spirit of the North; but he saw stagnation, too, and a looking-back to days that will not return

SOMETHING like a million people live on Tyneside, and most of them have never been to London—it costs a lot of money by train or bus, and by sea it takes about as long as it does to get to Hamburg. And anyway the Tynesider doesn't like travelling. He is proud of "the North," anything beyond York is "the South," and his capital is "canny Newcassel."

There is a lot of Scottish blood in the Tynesider, but "canny" doesn't mean to him what it does on Clydeside. It means something small and friendly and with a fascination of its own. And Newcastle, with its quarter of a million people, its quays, shipyards, sweet-factories, flour mills and markets, is always "canny" to the Tyneside Geordie.

Coming Up From The River

The changes in level provide fine views, allow the air that comes up from the river to circulate through the city.

Newcastle stands on the north side of the river—in the old days the Castle guarded the only bridge in those parts, and there is still no bridge or tunnel across the river on the ten-mile stretch from Newcastle to the sea—but along both sides of the river, all the way down to North and South Shields, and for some five miles upstream, there is nothing but slipways, quays, staithes, ropeworks, warehouses and all the variety of grimy prosperity and grimy stagnation.

The middle classes and the wealthy live in Gosforth and Jesmond, suburbs of Newcastle, or up the river at Hexham, or down on the coast at Whitley Bay. Geordie lives beside his work, or the place where he used to work. All the big stores, the business-men's clubs, the

The series centred on *His First Shift* (or *The Foreshift*), a painting of himself, as it were, aged fourteen, leaving the house in the dark with his mother on the doorstep seeing him off.

Oliver Kilbourn, 'A Boy's Day', *c.*1938

'It doesn't always happen that a lad makes his first start on an early morning shift, but I thought that by making him, in my picture, set off at dawn it would give more point to my story; but this did not actually occur to me until I was working on the panel itself,' he told Robert Lyon. 'I don't want anyone to think I have tried to make it look as if the idea of this young lad leaving home in the early morning is something tragic or terrific; neither do I ask anybody to be sorry for him or any of the other boys who start in the pits when they are fourteen. They are not a bit sorry for themselves. I have also tried to show by his jaunty air that he considered himself grown up and full of pluck . . .'

The 'Boy's Day' drawings, in pen and ink, go from being awakened to go on the 2 am foreshift to work down below, hanging full tubs on the 'trot' (endless rope), then home to bed, almost too tired to eat, so exhausted he sleeps through until his mother calls him again to get ready for work once more.

'It used to be creepy in the pit. You could hear little bits of things

going on: timber creaking, bits of stone dropping here and there. Until you got used to it you were frightened.'

Fear of the dark, of extinction, is one theme in 'A Boy's Day', but a stronger one is reminiscence, Kilbourn himself being the lad whose pride in becoming a breadwinner overcame his fear. More pit scenes, in pen and wash, followed from these small and eloquent sketches. Many years later they served as the outline for his 'My Life as a Pitman'.

'Unbeknown to the ordinary man,' said Harry Wilson, 'there's a heck of a lot going on; there's a great big industry down below.'[3] Tom Harrisson and Julian Trevelyan were taken down Ashington Colliery to see for themselves the world of long sloping galleries leading to the narrow extremes of the coal face where the pit props crowded them and the air smelt singed. Looking on, they could marvel at the remoteness and the sensation of being at some battlefront. It was easy to romanticise the daily struggle, to represent it entirely in terms of black and white, as George Orwell did:

'More than anything else, perhaps, the miner can stand as the type of the manual worker, not only because his work is so exaggeratedly awful,

Pen and ink drawings by Oliver Kilbourn: *Drilling Shot Hole, Firing Shot, Coalface Drawers, Ellington Pit Yard,* *c.*1939

but also because it is so vitally necessary and yet so remote from our experience, so invisible as it were that we are capable of forgetting it as we forget the blood in our veins.'[4]

Oliver Kilbourn and Jimmy Floyd, who spent almost their entire working lives underground, didn't quite see it that way. The necessity of it, yes, but not the exaggerated awfulness. 'I've spent shall we say about a third of my life in semi-darkness,' Kilbourn said, and his eyes

became attuned to subtleties where outsiders would see only gloom. Each shift was a hazard; each job involved strength and skills.

'The face now. You went in in the morning and it was very very low. Some seams here were just about two feet (there was one seam called the Yard Seam which seemed paradise compared with a two-foot seam). Well, you were on your knees or sometimes lying on your back or sideways, and you were jolly glad to get your legs stretched a bit.

Sometimes you might walk out to the main gateway to get your legs and body stretched a bit and then you'd go in again. Upon the whole, the getting of coal was so intense that you hadn't much time to think about other things really during your shift. In the days when you just had candles it was very gloomy: it used to look very spooky before the First World War, you know, before the improvements started to take place.

'Law forbids men to take risks now as they used to once upon a time. There's what they call a minimum wage which didn't exist then. If a man didn't go into his place and fill a certain number of tubs, well, he was poorly off, so therefore many a time he went into a place that was half full of water, too impatient to wait till it was drained, and got on with his job. The result was that he often took cold and pneumonia. If he didn't take these risks he was sometimes called a softy; you know it wasn't, but it was sometimes fear maybe of what his pals thought of him if he didn't do some of these things. Actually there were a lot of accidents due to risks, needless risks I would say.

'You were isolated. You were in a place hundreds of yards from anybody else excepting the putter lad going in every now and again, and

Andy Rankin, *Pit Accident*, 1938

TOP Oliver Kilbourn, *Ashington Colliery*, 1947
LEFT Jimmy Floyd, *The Miner*, *c*.1939
BELOW Jimmy Floyd, *The Onsetter*, *c*.1942

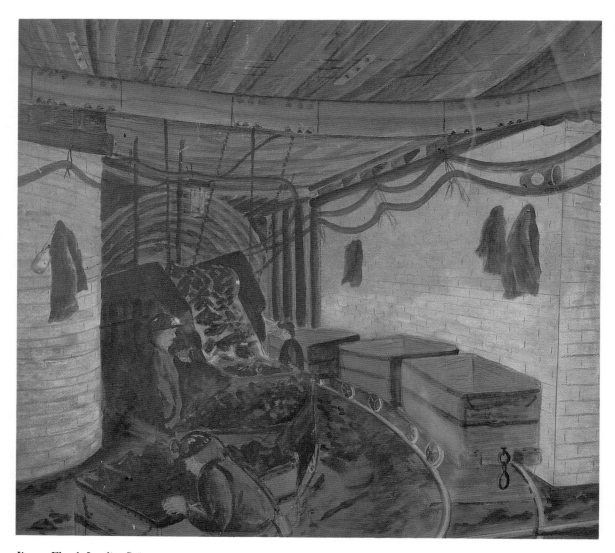

Jimmy Floyd, *Loading Point*, c.1942

Jimmy Floyd, *Bait Time*, 1946

Harry Wilson, *Registration*, 1940

OPPOSITE ABOVE Oliver Kilbourn, *North Street Corner*, 1947
OPPOSITE BELOW LEFT Oliver Kilbourn, *Building Shelters*, 1940
OPPOSITE BELOW RIGHT Oliver Kilbourn, *Spring '42*, 1942

TOP Oliver Kilbourn, *Coal Face Filler*, c.1945   BELOW Oliver Kilbourn, *Salvage Drawers*, 1945

TOP Len Robinson, *Spring Fever*, 1946   BELOW Len Robinson, *Washhouse*, 1950s

Len Robinson, *Rendez-Vous Cafe*, 1946

the Deputy. By law he had to make at least two inspections per shift and write a report out about what he saw. If there was any dangerous stone hanging or any gas about or anything like that, "Well," he would say, "now be careful of that right hand corner there. I don't like the look of that stone, I'd get a prop in and a plank." Alright, you'd say, I'll put it in, but when he went away we'd keep on filling these tubs and probably not bother about it. Well, sometimes you were very unfortunate and it maybe came down and lamed you or something. That was often happening.'[5]

Jimmy Floyd was an onsetter for many years, moving filled tubs into the cage and marshalling the empty ones. When there was an accident he would help put the victim into the cage with the two men holding the stretcher. Arthur Whinnom's *Pit Incident* shows the outcome. 'This is a fatal accident,' Floyd said. 'They used to come to the surface and take the stretchers out and the women used to rush to the scene to see who it was. But this is a fatal accident so the blanket's right over the face, you see.'

Harry Wilson remembered that when he was a boy and went to school in a mining village, 'the miners used to pass the gate of the school on the way home from work and on occasion a dead miner would be brought out of the pit and carried past the school gates and I remember vividly how all the children used to run forward to find out if it was their daddy or not. That has lived with me all my life.'

Experience gives to Jimmy Floyd's *Bait Time*, with its air of complicity as the pony reaches over to take a bit of jam sandwich, and to *The Onsetter*, with its detailed apparatus, a self-explanatory quality. Oliver Kilbourn's *Coal Face Filler*, *Cold Press* and *The Salvage Drawers*, done during the war, show the expertise needed to judge safety margins and also the mutual trust developed in a work team. *Pithead Baths*, on the other hand, celebrates the new amenities of the late Thirties: at Ellington Colliery an end to walking home dirty. Clothes were hauled above head height to keep them out of the way and prevent pilfering.

'I'm sick and tired of miners being portrayed like lumps of wood – all downtrodden with work,' Oliver Kilbourn said. 'We tried to bring realism to the portrayal. In some of my paintings that quality comes over: the miner is quite happy to get his work out and the putter lad is quite happy to supply his needs. Everything done to the extent of their ability.'

On 16 January 1939 the Group, led by Robert Lyon, took part in a North Regional broadcast instead of the usual Tuesday night meeting. 'Wansbeck' in the *Morpeth Herald* the following Friday reported the discussion at length. Robert Lyon began, and Harry Wilson and Arthur Whinnom made statements, after which *The Two Shifts* was discussed. The discussion was, it was stated, similar to that which takes place at

DAILY HERALD   JANUARY 16, 1939

MINERS WILL GIVE RADIO TALK ON ART

FOURTEEN working men, most of them miners, will tell the world to-night how they found an escape from the drabness of the colliery town in which they live by taking up painting as a hobby.

8.40 'THE PLEASURES OF PAINTING'

Confessions and criticisms by
The Ashington Group
Led by Robert Lyon

The Ashington Group is organised as a tutorial class from King's College, Newcastle-upon-Tyne, and meets every Monday night under the Master of Painting for discussion of work done during the week. Many of the members work in the colliery, others are insurance agents and teachers. None is a professional artist.

(Stagshaw)

They are members of the "Ashington Group," and they are to broadcast their work from the B.B.C.'s Newcastle (Stagshaw) studio.

The Ashington Group was formed at Newcastle more than two years ago by Mr. Robert Lyon, Master of Fine Art at King's College, Durham University.

At the little coal-mining town of Ashington its members meet frequently and paint, receiving technical guidance from Mr. Lyon.

"The paintings are not executed to be sold, but because we want to paint them and want to do it in our own way," say the members.

In the broadcast four members—a coal-face miner, a colliery joiner, a colliery blacksmith and a coal order clerk—will talk, and then the entire group will discuss a picture painted by one of their number.

the weekly classes of the group and there was a battle royal between the defenders of naturalism – or anti-distortionists – and those who favoured symbolical expression.

'The critics of the picture were sufficiently aggressive and dogmatic to make the wrangle interesting, for, strangely enough, the symbolists or champions of free expression of feeling were the more academic of the protagonists. There was a satisfying amount of cut and thrust in the argument, and although the defenders of naturalism and critics of distortion were obviously outnumbered, it was pleasing to hear one or two truculent voices expressing statements which were definitely "agin the Government".

'Perhaps in new movements and new trends of thought these days the old fashioned folk are the rebels.'

During the broadcast Robert Lyon asked Leslie Brownrigg, the pitman turned elementary school teacher, what his reaction was to the Group having a London exhibition. Brownrigg answered, 'It must be very difficult for people seeing the show to understand what we are getting at, and what we get out of it anyway. The atmosphere of an exhibition is all so different from the hut in which we meet, and the talk and discussion which goes on there. I don't rightly know, but it seems to me that to look at a painting by Jimmy Floyd without watching Jimmy at work on it, or knowing something about Jimmy himself, as we all do in the class, must mean that the painting loses a lot of its point.'

Mass Observation's Brian Allwood, reporting on the exhibition at Fulham Central Library, said he had the impression that 'most of those present were really interested in the paintings as something quite new in their lives. Half of them signed the list provided for names of people interested in the formation of art groups. Over half were working class, the rest shopkeeper and clerk type. No intellectual-looking people or art students.'[6]

But no art groups resulted. As Tom Harrisson said in his list of 'the necessary conditions for a successful group', a 'corporate spirit' was essential. 'All money from sale of pictures must be put into the group funds for general advancement of the class . . . no committee, decisions not put to any vote' (that, Harry Wilson commented years later, meant quite something). 'For four years the plan has worked well because all are united by a common interest. They get positive pleasure out of watching each other paint and enjoying each other's results. They enjoy especially the painting of Youngs, who says little, can't speak a word of BBC, always wears a cap.'[7]

That last detail was a Harrisson afterthought. He expected someone like Harry Youngs to be inseparable from his cloth cap. It went with the received picture of working class Britain especially north of the Black Country. Bill Brandt, for one, had brought back from Durham images of men in caps and mufflers scrabbling for coal on waste-tips and the memorable glimpse of the man wheeling a sackful of spoils over a drear moor. Humphrey Spender's Ashington wasn't anything like so grim, but he too found what he sought: a clannish society with caps on heads. Equally, in headlines everywhere except in the *Morpeth Herald* which, being local, knew better, the Ashington Group were usually referred to as 'miner artists', the implication being that they were all hewers and fillers, that when they weren't (cloth-capped) at their easels they were hacking at the coalface. Even Robert Lyon emphasised in his thesis that Oliver Kilbourn mixed soot with white distemper when he painted *His First Shift*, thereby blending the fruits of his labour with the medium of his art.

The romanticism of *The Stars Look Down*, combined with the prescriptive realism of those in the AIA and elsewhere who believed that 'ordinary' art could help provoke change, made the Group irresistible to well-wishers. The *Morpeth Herald*'s 1936 headline 'Art Pilgrimage to London' could now be reversed. The art pilgrimage to Ashington was for those who read *Left Review* and, subsequently, John Lehmann's *New Writing* hoping to enjoy worker-prose amidst the belles lettres and dialectic. 'Lots of people in Bloomsbury and the Garden Cities are on the look-out for the emergence of the proletarian writer,' remarked John Middleton Murry in *New Britain*, Autumn 1934. 'I have actually met one or two: real class-conscious proletarians with an authentic though imperfect gift of experience in the written word . . . A few days ago I met a proletarian writer, by appointment, in a great industrial city of the North . . . He wore an old cloth cap and a greasy raincoat.'[8]

This unnamed literary figure became one of many, among them MO's Bill Naughton, the Lancashire lorry-driver and short story writer; Sid Chaplin the Durham miner and North East novelist, and B. L. Coombes the Welsh miner whose autobiography *These Poor Hands* was published by the Left Book Club in 1939. All three were taken up by Lehmann. There was even a Conservative proletarian writer: G. A. W. Tomlinson, from the Nottinghamshire coalfield, whose *Coal Miner* was published by the National Book Association in 1937 with a preface by Arthur Bryant. A 'refreshing contrast', Bryant found it, to another book he had read recently. 'It was called *The Road to Wigan Pier* and was, I believe, one of the choices of the "Left Book Club". It was written by a young literary man of refined tastes who at some apparent inconvenience to himself had "roughed it" for a few weeks in Wigan and Sheffield.' While talking darkly about 'the difference between propaganda and reality', Bryant made one reasonable, if Panglossian observation: 'Though Wigan and Sheffield may perhaps genuinely seem Hell to a super-sensitive novelist paying them a casual visit, they do not seem Hell to the vast majority of people who live there'.

Tomlinson, it must be said, describes working conditions that the vast majority of people would have considered hellish. When he was an onsetter, for example:

'I used to be stiff with the cold, wet through with the water that is constantly falling down the shaft and half-blinded by the coal dust that blew back into my face each time the cages were loaded. From fifty to sixty times each hour this performance had to be gone through for the whole of the shift. It is unbelievably monotonous and wearying.'[9]

Shortly before the war Ashington Council decided to begin house-building on some of the allotments and thereby reduce the number of 'temporary dwellings' – vans, sheds, tents even – then in use. There were more than a hundred of these, by the Medical Officer's reckoning, more or less unfit for habitation. One of them, actually on the site to be cleared, was a large hut, fifteen feet by thirty-two, big enough the Group thought to serve as a weekend retreat and a bargain at £10. So they bought it, took it apart and had it moved to Long Horsley, about twelve miles away towards Rothbury and the hills.

The idea was that they would spend spare time there, idyllically

The Hut at Long Horsley,
1939: being erected and, later,
with Leslie Brownrigg's car

placed for landscape painting in a field beside a stream. The distance
was a drawback, admittedly, as only Leslie Brownrigg had a car and
their bicycles wouldn't be much use in the winter months. They went
ahead though. Mr Hammond, the Managing Director of the Coal
Company, let them have a thousand bricks for the foundations and they
calculated that the whole project – purchase, shifting and fitting out –
would cost them about £50 to £60: most of the proceeds of the
exhibitions. But then the war began, so they left the hut propped and
stayed, the door nailed up, for the duration.

8

'Hev' ye ony ideas t'help with the air-raid precautions?'
'Whaat aboot butterfly nets t'catch the bombs?'

Ashington Collieries Magazine

Mining was a reserved occupation, so even those members of the Group who were of military age had no call to leave Ashington, except for the ex-miner Leslie Brownrigg, and he was soon invalided out of the army with a stomach ulcer. For the first nine months of the war there wasn't even extra demand for coal. Output went down slightly, to a little under three million tons a year, though during the war the Ashington collieries actually contributed a fraction more than before to the production of Northumberland as a whole: up by one percent to twenty-five percent. Unemployment in Ashington fell from 1157 in 1939 to 306 in 1940 and 55 in 1941. There were some air raids but the only damage suffered was in Lynemouth and Newbiggin.[1]

The war meant Robert Lyon often failed to get to Ashington. Meetings were increasingly difficult to arrange because they could no longer count on being able to use the YMCA room. Besides, there were extra shifts to work and, on top of that, civil defence duties. Arthur Whinnom arranged the distribution of gas masks. Others joined the Fire Service and the Home Guard. Because he was a teacher, Edwin Harrison helped organise evacuees. His painting 'Evacuation' shows him in the classroom checking names on lists as children are mar-shalled, fed, kept in order and made to do gasmask practice while blackout curtains are being hung and, outside in the yard, shelters are hastily built. Oliver Kilbourn's *School Shelters* adds to the record. While workmen mix cement and lay bricks, boys drill at the far end of the playground. 'It's all there. I feel I know all about what's going on,' said Harry Wilson.

He too was keen to illustrate the impact of war on everyday life. 'The government issued everyone in the country with a registration number and I was one of the enumerators.' His painting *Registration* shows him calling on a household not in his usual role as an insurance man but as an official.

'My job was to go in and get a big sheet filled in for each person in the

Edwin Harrison, *Evacuation*, 1940

house. Well, it was quite a job in some of these houses because, as this picture indicates, four generations were in the one house, which illustrates the overcrowding there was in those days. It's a colliery house with four rooms only. On the left there's a son with his wife and two children. In the background there's the old lady mending a pair of socks and the father and mother too. Two younger sons in the foreground, and that's me with a grey hat on, filling in the census form giving them their numbers. See, the light's shaded to prevent the light shining outside.'[2]

The Group now engaged on its own programme of war art. As it happened, the man who, under Sir Kenneth Clark, ran the War Artists' Advisory Committee (dedicated, Clark argued, to keeping artists alive and occupied and useful) was Robert Lyon's predecessor at Armstrong College, E. M. O'Rourke Dickey. Thirty years later Dickey was to claim he had started the Ashington Group in 1927, a claim based it would seem on some confusion since there is no record of a WEA course on art in Ashington run by anyone but Robert Lyon and no mention of Dickey occurs in the Group's archive. However, as secretary of the Ministry of Information committee Dickey was in a position to foster the sort of art with which the Ashington Group could identify: reportage based on observation and experience rather than abstract notions.[3]

The general level of the Official War Art produced was, Kenneth Clark said, 'mediocre and tame'. While the RAF element on the committee pressed for pictures of Spitfires in action and the Army thought more in terms of rip-roaring ground combat and portraits suitable for regimental headquarters, he contrived to find work for the artists he favoured, among them Graham Sutherland and, especially, Henry Moore.

'The ultimate difference between amateur and professional is that the latter does not need the spur of a sudden external stimulus,' wrote the critic Eric Newton in his introduction to *War Through Artists' Eyes*, a picturebook published in 1945, by which time the stimulus had gone and the War Art was being distributed to provincial, national and Commonwealth galleries or put into store at the Imperial War Museum.[4]

'The professional works on the momentum he has gradually built up during a lifetime of labour, whereas the amateur, possibly equally gifted, often more sensitive, has to start each time from scratch.'

Clark and Dickey must have agreed with Newton for certainly Sutherland and Piper sketching Blitz damage, Paul Nash imagining enemy bombers with shark's teeth, Edward Ardizzone jovial among the troops, were gratifyingly professional. Their styles prevailed. Amateurs

Oliver Kilbourn, *Grand Hotel*, 1941

Henry Moore, *Miner Pushing Tubs*, 1942

could submit work to the Committee but they could hardly compete. Others, many of them commercial artists in the Auxiliary Fire Service, who took part in Fireman Artists' exhibitions, had plenty to stimulate them but theirs wasn't the sort of art Clark manoeuvred for. He wanted transcendence, in fairly advanced terms, a wish echoed by Eric Newton when he said, 'The record must give way to symbols.'

Henry Moore who, Sir Kenneth used to remark, would have made an ideal representative of the human race on some other planet, realised single-handed his patron's war art aims, first with his underground shelter drawings, begun in September 1940, and then with the coal-mining series based on sketches made the following year during two weeks spent at Wheldale Colliery, Castleford, where his father had once worked. 'If one was asked to describe what Hell might be like, this would do,' he wrote to Alan Wilkinson, his drawings cataloguer, many years later. 'A dense darkness you could touch, the whirring din of the coal-cutting machine . . .'[5]

Moore's miners and sleepers, worked up into effigies, were taken to symbolise victimisation and dumb, yet noble, toil. They are impressive as entombments, mummifications even but, Oliver Kilbourn thought, 'he misses part out. His pit drawings are not of real live miners because he did not understand what was about. I could not help but contrast the lively sketches that Rodin did for his sculptures and look what it did for his sculpture – full of mood, liveliness, movement and drama. Right from the beginning Moore's drawings were static, because he made them as statues, therefore they remained lifeless, like his sculpture.'

A few years later the Group was to invite Henry Moore to come and talk to them; in the meantime Oliver Kilbourn proceeded with his

Harry Wilson, *Wartime Wedding*, 1940

Arthur Whinnom, *Gas Mask for Baby*, 1941

Harry Wilson, *War at Sea*, 1941

studies of precise tasks and conditions underground. Harry Wilson painted a war-time wedding, the bride and groom (in battledress) entering the photographer's shop for what might prove to be the only tangible reminder of a brief marriage. His *War at Sea*, more overtly symbolic, is a beleaguered foreshore where boats – one of them the 'Belgie' – have been washed up by a heavy sea. The painting carries intimations of what, in the South, was becoming known as Neo-Romanticism. Arthur Whinnom too showed panic mixed with foreboding in his *Gas Mask for the Baby*.

'We had been talking of Goya and his pictorial comments on war – a discussion which was cut short by an air raid warning,' Robert Lyon wrote. 'This raid happened at a time when there was a good deal of apprehension about the possible use of gas, and masks for babies were not being supplied in very large numbers. It was Whinnom's job to see these masks fitted and their use explained; but the fact that there were so few to be distributed, and panic was not very far away, made a deep impression on him which he has "got out of himself" as he says, in a way which owes nothing to Goya's bitter criticisms though both artists have been keenly aware of a grim and moving tragedy.'[6] Whinnom put

Photograph of the Group at work, *c.*1941. Left to right: unknown, J. R. Dobson, G. Brown, O. Kilbourn, J. Floyd, A. Rankin, H. Youngs

his hand in the foreground, showing how to pump air into the container, the baby struggling, the parents helpless.

In November 1940 news came from Long Horsley that the hut, which they had handed over to the Army the previous August, had been damaged in a gale. They found it half-wrecked, blown off its foundations. Apparently the door had been left open and cattle had taken to using it as a byre. A complaint to the police in Morpeth and referral to the District Claims Officer got them nowhere, for the Army denied having requisitioned the hut and told them to consider the damage an 'act of God'. Arthur Whinnom launched into a correspondence that wasn't satisfactorily resolved for two years.

'One of the terrible things about modern war is that it not only destroys lives and treasure, but that it threatens to dry up the very springs of civilization and wither the seed beds of the humanities – the nurseries of religion, scholarship, art and manners,' Helen Sutherland wrote in her introduction to the catalogue of the Group's second exhibition at the Laing Art Gallery, in June 1941. 'It is therefore a matter of deep satisfaction that in spite of longer and more strenuous working hours and arduous civil defence duties, the Ashington Group is still very much alive, and that its members have made rather than found time to continue their classes and bring forth a fresh wealth of inspired and original work.'

The exhibition was opened by Lady Ridley. She had rather expected, 'Wansbeck' reported in the *Morpeth Herald*, to be 'confronted with dreary paintings and pretty water-colours. She had however been amazed by what she had seen and there were a great many of the paintings she wanted to possess.'

'These pictures are to my mind encouraging. They represent an outlook on life which is fresh and spontaneous. At the same time they are the work of mature minds, of men who have lived fully and felt deeply, and have something to express. That is a quality which is becoming exceedingly rare.'[7]

Lady Ridley concluded by inviting the Group to tea at Blagdon Hall, to see the pictures there, and the house and gardens. Leslie Brownrigg thanked her and added that the war had failed to break up the class and that in seven years they had grown in friendship under the guidance and inspiration of Robert Lyon.

This was reflected in the paintings on show, more than a hundred, of which many were portraits. As 'Wansbeck' explained, 'the painters have tried to represent themselves or their colleagues by depicting their interests and environments. Thus, by getting rid of the face, the painter gets closer to the man himself. The portraits are anonymous but even to a person unfamiliar with the members these interesting experiments give a lively insight into the lives of the subjects. A violin and a piece of

At work in the Hut. Left to right: unknown, J. R. Dobson, G. Brown

music show that the man is something of a musician, a room containing cases of stuffed birds and a gun reveal the sportsman, walking boots and a glimpse of the mountains show that the subject is a wanderer in the hills, half-filled paint pots, brushes and a hunk of bread in a newspaper depict the house-painter and an untidy house with dirty pans in the fireplace show the man whose wife is away on holiday.

'Employing similar techniques, one exhibitor (Oliver Kilbourn) contrives to crowd into his picture every inanimate object representative of the confined and arduous life of a working-man's wife. This painting, *My Mother*, shows us the fireplace with a row of formidable loaves "rising" on the hearth – evidently a large family – the baking board, rolling pin and dough on the table, washing on the line. Everything is there except the woman herself, but there is sufficient to set the imagination at work reconstructing the figure of a mother working ceaselessly and tirelessly for her men-folk, seven days a week and 18 hours a day.

'A memorable self-portrait is that of a colliery undermanager (Gavin Milne) who sees modern coal production as a nightmare of coal tubs converging remorselessly and everlastingly upon the manager's desk, where coals even fill the wastepaper basket.

'The war pictures include barrage balloons over familiar localities, searchlights cutting lanes of light through the night sky, wardens

Oliver Kilbourn, *All Clear*, 1941

rushing to their duty posts at the sounding of the "alert" and rushing home again at the "all clear", the process of fitting on gas masks at a warden's post, reception of evacuees at a school, a war-time wedding and war-time parting, a family listening to crisis news on the radio, a mother watching over her children who sleep during an air-raid "alert".'[8]

Most of these paintings have disappeared, but from this description and from the titles listed in the catalogue it is obvious that the guiding theme was the impact of war. There were a few ventures into a grander manner (*War at Sea* rather looks as though it was composed during a Churchill broadcast), but for the most part the pictures were to do with irksome restrictions, blackout and anxiety. In Ashington most air-raid warnings led to nothing, but one never knew; as it was, during the Summer of 1941 Northumberland miners were widely criticised for not going to work during alerts, unlike the miners of County Durham.

Mass Observation, retained by the Ministry of Information to report on public attitudes and morale, could have used the Laing exhibition as a body of evidence, a complete dossier of preoccupations, from Andy Rankin's *Pit Accident* to Leslie Brownrigg's *War in the Lake District* in which a Wordsworthian wandered with his gasmask. Sir Kenneth Clark and E. M. O'R. Dickey may have noticed Oliver Kilbourn's *School Shelters* reproduced one week in *The Listener*, but if they did they made no enquiries about this unofficial war art. It was outside their province.

'Wansbeck', however, appreciated how the Group had come on in just a few years. 'Compared with the first, shy, hesitant appearance of the Group some years ago, the new exhibition is a strong, confident affair. There is still some faulty drawing, about which there was so much adverse comment in the early days of the experiment, but now ideas and conceptions come out fairly firmly, compelling attention in that only the idea and feeling of the painter's experiment matter.

'One street scene has a slight propagandist tendency – but it is good propaganda, for it shows a street in a pit village with an open sewer down the middle. North Seaton is recognisable.

'One well-dressed individual, examining the picture, observed "That sort of thing ought to be done away with". So the propaganda is effective.'[9]

Thirteen members of the Group, with Robert Lyon, went over to Blagdon Hall, ten miles away in feudal Northumberland, a couple of weeks after the exhibition opening. Most of them cycled there and had their photo taken resting by the roadside en route. Lady Ridley had bought three of their paintings: George Brown's *My Uncle*, Oliver Kilbourn's *Saturday Morning* and Harry Wilson's *Two Shifts*. They posed with her for a more formal photograph outside on the terrace, flanked by two ornamental putti.

It was now, after the best part of seven years with the Group, that Robert Lyon gave serious thought to what had been achieved. His MA thesis, 'The Appreciation of Art Through the Visual and Practical Approach', was completed in April 1942, a couple of months before he was offered the job of Principal of Edinburgh College of Art.

Among the '"home-made" principles' he lists, the most important to him was that 'Exercises in technique are not to be considered as picture-making in the permanent or exhibition sense.' And while he

Photograph of Group members on their way to Blagdon Hall; left to right: G. Brown, H. Wilson, J. Floyd, G. Brownrigg, L. Brownrigg, unknown, O. Kilbourn

insists that 'these paintings have never been shown in clubs, Art Galleries in London and in the provinces without reference being made to the conditions under which they were produced,' he has to admit that 'by putting themselves in the place of the artist and so establishing emotional sympathy', the members of the Group became distanced from 'art-lovers' and, in effect, became artists themselves.

Lyon clearly preferred paintings that best illustrated his thesis, Harry Youngs' *Dawn*, for example. 'Youngs has not drawn upon a store of knowledge outside his own experience to fill up his picture; he knows about cocks and hens and what a hen-run looks like at dawn, just as he knows about cottage gardens, growing leeks and pit ponies. This picture is part of his life as he knows and feels it. He describes the time when the idea begins to show up as the most exciting part of the whole job. "Then," he says, "you forget about the war and everything else; your hands move faster and more easily, almost as if they were out of control".'[10]

On 28 July 1942, Lyon wrote to Arthur Whinnom: 'Just a line now to break the news of my departure in September for Edinburgh . . . I will write to you more fully later and will see you all on my return in three weeks' time, but for the moment I would like to assure you of my regrets at this break in our association of eight years; what a break it will be and I shall look back on it with feelings of deep gratitude for the satisfaction and help it has given me. I am rather tired and must have a few days holiday before seeing our show launched in an expectant art world. Tout à vous, Robert Lyon.'[11]

The show Lyon refers to was at the Lefevre Galleries: thirty-three paintings priced at between £8 and £25. Four were sold. A. J. McNeill Reid, who had given L. S. Lowry his first one-man exhibition in 1939, saw the Group as somewhat similar: painters whose originality lay in their amateurism, whose paintings could not be seen – in Robert Lyon's phrase – without 'reference being made to the conditions under which they were produced'. Jan Gordon's catalogue introduction emphasised this. He quoted a recent piece in *The Observer* about 'Ashington at Work and at Play' in which the Group had been mentioned.

'"Dooant goo up and tell them it's an easy life," said an underground filler, laughing at the correspondent. Well, look at Brownrigg's expressive picture of just such a brawny man cramped in a narrow seam . . . and then imagine yourself after work going home and studying art and art appreciation in your leisure . . .'[12]

At least two of the paintings that were sold, Arthur Whinnom's *The Family Pig* (£12) and Jimmy Floyd's *My Grandfather's Hobby* (£25), had an innocent appeal. The Floyd in particular was charming: 'an imaginary peep,' Robert Lyon described it, 'at this canary breeder with his prize certificates nailed to the wall, his chair temporarily vacated, the arrangements of the bird medicines and disinfectant, breeding cages and food boxes'.

There were only a couple of paintings by Oliver Kilbourn at the Lefevre, which rather suggests his wasn't the sort of approach favoured by McNeill Reid: too articulate to be safely classified 'naïve'. As Percy Horton, writing under the pseudonym 'Toros' in *Left Review* in April 1938 had observed, 'Since the discovery of Henri Rousseau – the French customs officer – there has been a growing interest in the productions of "Sunday artists" – and not only on the part of art

Jimmy Floyd, *My Grandfather's Hobby*, 1937

specialists. The upholders of the present social system have not been slow to recognise the value of encouraging workers to draw and paint at evening "Institutes" and the arrangement by big industrial concerns of exhibitions and competitions for art produced by their employees – these are examples of the sort of encouragement which has been given ... The Sunday painter is encouraged to be a harmless little man absorbed in what Cézanne once called 'sa petite sensation' and oblivious to the social questions agitating his fellow men.'[13]

Horton, who had done a lot of volunteer teaching at the Working Men's College in St Pancras, was in 1942 combining teaching at the Royal College of Art, evacuated to Ambleside, with Westmorland Home Guard activities and a few War Art commissions, among them portrait drawings of select Home Front personalities such as Fireman Turner of Hull, and, more ambitious, *Blind Men Working on War Production, Lucas Factory, Birmingham*. Horton was a solid professional with no time for those who pandered to lightweight tastes. His *Left Review* strictures had lost some of their pertinence by 1942, yet it was undeniable that 'Sunday painting', whether at Mrs Wertheim's gallery or at the Lefevre, was there because it was taken to be amusingly sincere or, as Lady Ridley said, 'fresh and spontaneous'. And, therefore, a good filler for commercial premises in the dog days of the war. The Lefevre was later bombed out.

On 2 October Robert Lyon, newly installed in Edinburgh, wrote to Arthur Whinnom as Secretary of the Group, telling him that he had succeeded in arranging for the Lefevre pictures to be taken to Edinburgh and shown at the National Gallery of Scotland, available because its own collection was elsewhere for safekeeping. He proposed adding Helen Sutherland's paintings (in the event she ignored his request: since 1939 she had been living in the Lake District) and Lady Ridley's, plus more recent work if possible. 'Don't forget,' he added, 'that though I am some distance away from you now, my interest is as strong, if not stronger than when I was with you.' Eleven of the Group went up to Edinburgh for the opening. 'Here we have a group of adults finding self-expression,' said the Director of the National Gallery, the former Scottish Futurist Stanley Cursiter, 'under conditions which may be compared with the recent exhibition of work by Boys' Clubs.'

Already, at the Lefevre Galleries, the Ashington pictures, as Jan Gordon pointed out in *The Studio*, had been 'rather quaintly contrasted' with an autumn selection of 'French Paintings' (the Lefevre's stock in trade): Van Gogh's *Oliviers*, Picasso's *Oeufs*, a Corot, a Cézanne, a Manet and two Renoirs. Between these and the Scottish Boys' Clubs, the Group was in danger of being squeezed into a corner. Already they were attempting to find a buyer for their abandoned hut. Without Robert Lyon's 'guidance and inspiration' it was quite possible their experiment would come to an end.

9

*The war has caused us to revise our sense of values. We have
begin to feel that behind all those acute but temporary urgencies
that crowd in upon every moment of our lives there lies a set of
more permanent, more real demands that only art can satisfy.*

ERIC NEWTON *Art For Everybody*, 1943

The dispute over the damage done to the hut at Long Horsley was
revived in November 1942 when Arthur Whinnom wrote again to the
County Police in Morpeth. The replies were evasive. 'The hut was in
no different condition after the Military and the Police took an interest
in it than it had been before,' argued Captain Bancroft for the District
Claims Commission. Besides, he said, 'it has been definitely established from information received from the Police Authorities that the
Military did not, in fact, take possession of the property.' He advised
the Group to consider the entire incident an 'act of God'.

There was detailed rebuttal of this from Arthur Whinnom and
eventually, in April 1943, he was able to write to the Estates Manager of
the Ashington Coal Company asking a favour:

'During the last year or so we have found it increasingly difficult to
get a room in Ashington which we could use practically. At the present
moment we cannot do any work except in our own homes. I have to
explain that our hut at Longhorsley was intended to be a centre for
weekend landscape painting, and was taken over by the military. It
suffered damage whilst under their care and has since been returned to
us together with payment of compensation.

'If you could provide us with a site anywhere suitable in Ashington on
the Company's land so that we can carry on we shall indeed be grateful.
We would see to it that the hut presented a good clean appearance after
erection.'[1]

A site was found next to the Veterans' Institute in Hirst Yard behind
the Central Hall. The Coal Company charged 10/- a year ground rent.
In July they were given the go-ahead and began laying the foundations
and reassembling the walls and roof. They added a proper chimney and
a storage room at the back. Electricity was installed, paid for by a new
member, John Jenkins, a conscientious objector who had been sent to

Ashington to run a training face. His family owned a mining machinery firm. He didn't stay long and, after the war, he was killed in a climbing accident in the Alps.

A different era began for the Group. Already, in March, they had held an exhibition at the Miners' Welfare Institute. No longer could they be described as a Tutorial Class. Now that they had permanent premises, several new members besides John Jenkins, and a reputation to maintain, they saw themselves as an Ashington institution. They were also confident of being part of a growing movement, already looking to the post-war period, whenever that was to be.

'What is interesting,' Eric Newton remarked in 'Art For Everybody', a *Britain Advances* pamphlet published by the British Council in 1943, 'and what was, four years ago, quite unexpected, is the discovery that the war, far from interfering with our progress towards this better world, has actually pushed us a little nearer to it.'

Art for the People had entered a fresh phase. 'More efficient galleries throughout the country, more efficient art education for the rising generation, a closer connection between artist and manufac- turer, and closer contact between the artist and his public – all these things,' Newton said, 'are in the minds of the post-war planners, even though the full realization of them may seem difficult.' Firm on its foundations and with 'Ashington Art Group' written up over the door, the hut was an outpost of the Second Front of the arts in England.

In 1940 the organisation of the 'Art for the People' scheme, previously run by the British Institute of Adult Education, was taken over by the Council for the Encouragement of Music and the Arts. Exhibitions were circulated, with guide-lecturers to enthuse and explain and gauge reactions. Existing arts clubs were used as welcoming committees. The spread of enlightenment by such means became a wartime policy, a propaganda aim, best illustrated perhaps by Humphrey Jennings in two of his films for the Ministry of Information, *Listen to Britain* (1942) and *A Diary for Timothy* (1944–5) during which lunchtime crowds study war art in the National Gallery and Myra Hess plays Mozart in another room, the camera nosing in to reveal, among the very ordinary audience, Queen Elizabeth and Sir Kenneth Clark, smiling faintly.

A report on 'The Arts in England' by B. Ivor Evans and Mary Glasgow, published in 1949, conveys the out-reach attitude:

'From the point of view of the community itself, a vigorous arts club can be a channel to make known local needs and wishes and to draw up a programme for each season which shall be well balanced and acceptable . . . It must be said immediately, however, that this conception of its functions by an arts club can be exceedingly irritating to the London organiser.

'There is a danger, which it would be wrong to ignore, that a local society may come to form an exclusive circle limiting artistic activities to a certain section of the community represented by its members . . . Human nature being what it is, it may even be that a jealous arts club may actually wish to keep out the ordinary citizen who is not one of its original members.'[2]

Several exhibitions were sent to Ashington by the CEMA, to whom the North East was Region 1. In October 1943, 'Paintings and Drawings from the Collection of Wyndham Vint Esq.,' were shown: Sickert, Bomberg, Vlaminck, Fitton. The following March, 'Drawings and Water Colour Drawings' were exhibited at the Miners' Welfare, with Pamela Strain as guide-lecturer. The bulk of the works came from the Laing and the Shipley Art Gallery, Gateshead, but Lady Ridley lent an Epstein drawing of Epping Forest and two John Pipers: *Cale Cross at Blagdon* and *Seaton Delaval Hall*. Examples of the work of Robert Lyon, *Sussex Farm House* and *Farm House at Allerwash*, were provided by Arthur Whinnom and George Brownrigg.

'Art is not a popular subject in adult education,' reported the Arts Enquiry, a committee set up in 1941 by the Dartington Hall Trustees. Its survey 'The Visual Arts', published in March 1946, singled out the Ashington Group:

'A number of scattered adult education groups have individually engaged in painting and handicrafts; these include the Whitechapel Group in London, a WEA group at Haslemere and a smaller group at Barrow-in-Furness. But the most interesting of such groups is the Ashington Group in Northumberland.' The importance of the tutor was stressed, and also the inexplicable factors. 'The teacher chiefly responsible for the great success of the Ashington Group was unable to

Oliver Kilbourn, *Portrait of George Brown*, 1947

start similar classes in neighbouring towns and villages. In part this Group's success was due to the fact that it had met for many years previously in the study of other subjects, and was therefore a homogeneous group with long experience of working together.'

Two months after this official recognition, on Sunday 5 May, there was a special meeting of the Group to confirm a set of rules. This move was largely the doing of George Brown as President and Arthur Whinnom as Hon. Secretary. The aim was to get things straight. Once printed in a little pink booklet, the rules would distinguish the Group from sketch clubs and the like. Rules represented the Group's coming of age; its independence.

George Brown was particularly keen on having a rule-book to consult. Always somewhat cantankerous, he used to lay down the law to such effect that Jimmy Floyd more than once stormed out of the hut. Seven pages of regulations were thought up. Most of the clauses were to do with committee powers, subscriptions and so on. Robert Lyon and Helen Sutherland were made Life Honorary Members. Lapsed members were ordered to hand their hut keys in, qualifying for 1/- refund, while Article 7, 'Misdemeanour of a Member', stated that 'The Group shall cause to be brought before it any member whose conduct shall have been deemed to have been detrimental to the good name of the Group.'

A member could claim 'as his own property his particular work before going to exhibition, or before being hung upon the walls of the Group's Hut. Unless a member places a stated value upon his work it may be disposed of for a nominal sum and the money received shall be equally distributed between the artist and Group funds.' Article 19 concerned the Permanent Collection: 'The Group shall from time to

4.—Membership

The Group shall consist of the present members and others who may be admitted to membership under rule 5.

5.—New Members

To be informed when starting of the following conditions :

(1) A probation period which shall constitute 6 consecutive meetings;

(2) That the Group shall decide, at the 7th meeting, by unanimous vote, whether or not the candidate shall be accepted;

(3) The secretary shall notify the result to the candidate;

(4) If accepted, his fee for that year shall be pro rata.

6.—Members Lapsing

Any member who lapses shall hand in his key to the Group Hut and will receive refund of the 1/- charged for the key.

7.—Misdemeanour of a Member

The Group shall cause to be brought before it any member whose conduct shall have been deemed to have been detrimental to the good name of the Group, and to hear any explanation given by the said member.

The Group's decision shall be binding except for the right of a member to present his explanation to a " Special Meeting."

8.—Annual Subscription

The annual subscription shall be fixed at the annual meeting, which shall be held on the 1st regular meeting night in February.

All members to be fully paid up by the 31st March.

9.—Notice for Annual Meeting

The Secretary shall notify each member at least 14 days before the date of the annual meeting.

10.—End of the Financial Year

The financial year shall end on the 31st December.

11.—Annual Meeting

The annual meeting shall be held on the first regular meeting night in February. The Secretary and Treasurer shall each submit a report.

12.—Officers

To be elected annually at the annual meeting.

(1) President—to act as chairman at all meetings of the Group.

time desire and accept for purposes of acquiring a representative and permanent collection of work done by any of its members.'

The most important article however was No. 3: 'Aims and Objects'.

'The aim of the Group shall be the cultivation and appreciation of the Fine Arts by the following means:

a) To encourage the creation of works of art by the members;

b) The periodical exhibition of such work;

c) To associate with bodies having similar aims and objects;

d) To promote lecture programmes of a broad cultural interest on the Fine Arts;

e) Arranging visits of contemporary artists;

f) Building up a well-stocked library of books and reproductions;

g) Building up a representative and permanent collection of members' works of art (subject to the approval of the artist).'

The Rules clarify the Group's re-orientation. Now the main aim was to paint, exhibit and promote Ashington Group ideals. The Hut made it possible to start regarding the works produced as more than exercises; the permanent collection was its deposit account and the talk of a 'well-stocked library' was a declaration of intent. In future, as and when, the Group would have all the resources it needed.

Eight years before, in the discussions with Tom Harrisson before the Bensham Grove weekend, the list of ten requirements for a successful group had an entirely different emphasis. Then it was 'No committee, decisions not put to any vote'. Then, it was assumed a tutor would be required, 'a tutor who comes from outside, and so acts as a focus for the group, and makes outside decisions'.

Under Rule 3(e), ('visits of contemporary artists') lurked the memory of disappointment the previous summer when, presumably through the CEMA, they were provided with £40 as a fee for a lecture from some well-known artist. This was made available in May 1945, a few weeks before the founding of the Arts Council was announced; the grant was to be introductory in two senses: it was to bring the Group into contact with a notable professional, and it was to establish the principle that, in post-war Britain, Arts funding was to be for widespread benefit. Having consulted Robert Lyon and Helen Sutherland, the Group decided to ask Graham Sutherland, or Henry Moore or John Piper. Graham Sutherland wrote back expressing his admiration for the Group. He regretted that he wouldn't be able to come up to Ashington for some months at least. Henry Moore had three reasons for not being able to come either. He too admired the Group's efforts but it so happened he was fully occupied until the following year. Then perhaps.[3] The grant lapsed.

With the end of the war, the return of a Labour government in July 1945 and the nationalization of the coal-mines which came into effect in January 1947, it appeared that prospects had altered for good.

Oliver Kilbourn, *Cold Press*, 1945

'Almost the only black spot on the Home Front during the war has been the coal industry,' Harold Wilson remarked in his *New Deal for Coal* published in 1945. Nationalization, though important, was no cure-all. 'To say that the workers have responsibility because the State bears it . . . is to talk entirely in abstract, theoretical terms,' wrote J. B. Pick in *Under the Crust*, his account of eighteen months spent as a coal-miner in the Midlands during the war. 'This responsibility is not personal and is, therefore, meaning less as far as the miners are concerned. They have no use for abstractions and theories. They are interested in wages and conditions and self-respect.'[4]

The Ashington Coal Company had always been concerned with its public image; early on, the Quakers among the owners had established the Welfare Department and had seen to it that few pubs were allowed in the district. The *Ashington Collieries Magazine* ceased publication with nationalization. Immediate advantages may not have been as obvious in Ashington as in other parts of the country, but paid holidays, more investment in equipment, the provision of work tools (previously bought and paid for by the pitman himself) and improved health and safety regulations were immediate results of the hand-over to the National Coal Board. It was estimated that Ashington's coal reserves would last at least a century. The future seemed secure.

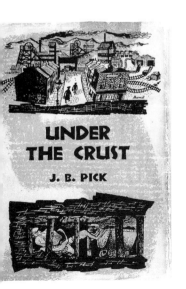

UNDER THE CRUST

J. B. PICK

There was also, for the first time, employment opportunity for women. In September 1945 an industrial estate at North Seaton was proposed. A women's clothing factory was established there in 1947 and, shortly after that, a cake decorations plant. No other firms were attracted to the Jubilee Trading Estate for some years, but with an electrical switchgear company nearby and Proudlocks the bakery, there was, by the mid-Fifties, a total of about nine hundred factory jobs, mostly for women, in the area. To some extent women were freed from domestic tasks by the new amenities. Pithead baths and pit canteens did away with the old end-of-shift routines and, given piped water and proper drainage, life became somewhat easier.[5]

For the Group, adjusting to circumstances, Rule 3 (c) proved a problem. 'Bodies having similar aims and objects' were anything from the Durham and District Art Society – and other AIA affiliates – to the Arts Council and the WEA. It was easy for the Group to slip into friendly relations with all the other exhibiting bodies in the region; in effect to associate with the sketch clubs and painting courses. In June 1946 they took part in an exhibition of work by living artists in the Northern Counties at the Laing. They were regarded as the mining contingent, with Oliver Kilbourn's *Coal Face Filler* singled out for mention. But they knew that theirs was a different set-up: they knew it and Robert Lyon had urged them in his letters to remember it. Writing to them in April 1945 he had described reactions to a broadcast he had given the previous January in 'London Calling' on the overseas service of the BBC.

'The broadcast appears to have gone down pretty well and the Ministry of Information is also using "*The* Group" intensively as part of their propaganda – In fact, I with many other people, KNOW that ASHINGTON IS IMPORTANT – and it is up to you all to keep your chins up – I MISS YOU ALL and look back on those evenings as *high-lights* in an otherwise not uninteresting life – and I can never thank you all enough for such friendliness.'[6]

Lyon's broadcast was reprinted as 'Miner Artists' in *La Nacion* of Argentina in July 1945 and as 'Coal Miner Artists' in *Victory*, the weekly magazine for India Command, a month later. One of the illustrations to George Orwell's 'The English People' in the *Britain in Pictures* series produced by Adprint was George Brownrigg's *Dawn* (*A Roadman, Early Morning*), here on a par with a Lowry street scene, a watercolour by F. C. Jones of the Great North Road at Castleford, and a Henry Moore drawing *Miners at the Pit Head*. Orwell talked of the need to do away with class distinctions and of the 'philistinism of the English public', their 'downright contempt for "cleverness"', their 'unawareness that aesthetic considerations can possibly have any importance'. James Boswell's response – typical AIA – in *The Artist's Dilemma*, published the same year, 1947, was 'it is the community's responsibility to demand that its representatives make it possible for the artist to paint and to carve those dreams and visions which enrich the present and predict the future.'[7]

Interest in the Group was now focussed not on its art educational uniqueness but on its contribution, so to speak, to 'Britain in Pictures'.

Paintings
by
THE ASHINGTON GROUP

AUGUST 7th—AUGUST 29th
1942

Foreword by
JAN GORDON

ALEX. REID & LEFEVRE, LTD.
(THE LEFEVRE GALLERIES)
1a KING STREET, ST. JAMES'S, S.W. 1

At a time when the British Council was commissioning the photographer J. Allen Cash to find archetypal English communities to photograph in order to project the image of a land of unchanging values and time-honoured ways in countries overseas, the Ashington 'Art for Everyone' (as it was described by Christopher Cross of the BBC's New York office, in an article for the *New York Times*) was another sort of 'Recording Britain'. Where the 'Recording Britain' project was a form of outdoor relief for topographic artists, initiated by Kenneth Clark and paid for by the Pilgrim Trust, Ashington painting was seen as being uniquely inspired and uniquely placed.

This was recognised by the National Coal Board when, prompted by the Arts Council, its Manpower and Welfare Department put on an 'Art by the Miner' exhibition, shown first in London in October 1947 and then, from April 1948 to March 1949, toured to Wolverhampton, Bristol, Stoke-on-Trent, Doncaster, Sunderland, Newcastle (the Laing again), Middlesbrough, Edinburgh, Dundee, Aberdeen, Glasgow and Belfast.

Paintings were included by miners from the Welsh and Yorkshire coalfields. Norman Cornish, of Dean and Chapter Colliery in County Durham, showed *The Pony Putter*: Cornish was to become the best-known miner-artist of the Fifties and Sixties, the only one to turn professional. A third of the exhibition, however, was a 'Group Exhibit by the Ashington Art Group', introduced as 'one collection of paintings related to one another rather than as individually selected works'.

Here, with a flourish, the Ashington Group took precedence. The nationwide tour was a sort of victory circuit. The paintings they showed were mostly from the Permanent Collection. 'Art by the Miner' was a setting in which they alone represented a sense of purpose beyond self-expression. As Oliver Kilbourn said later, 'We've been quite content to go our own way. We wanted our independence: if we had been fostered by other bodies we might have lost that.'[8] The Group had no desire to be identified as representative or exemplary Northerners. Indeed, as the Arts Council's professionalism developed, they lost contact with it and, in the early Fifties, they refused to associate with the Federation of Northern Art Societies. 'I agree with the lads', Robert Lyon wrote, 'And though I know very little about the Federation I always suspect over-organisation.' He no longer thought in terms of Ashington Groups elsewhere; and he saw no virtue in unprofessional jamborees. 'Ashington does not need the stimulant of association with other groups – or sketch clubs: I've always snooted at the amateur painter – there is no such thing – and sketch clubs have never produced anything worthwhile.'[9]

Instead the Group set about organising its own extra activities. In January 1948 they took part in a weekend course in modelling in clay from life at King's College, Newcastle. Photographs were published in the Newcastle *Evening Chronicle* and the *Sunday Sun* of sculpting in progress with the nude model posed next to an electric fire. It was hardly an Ashington Group occasion: far too conventionally artistic. The following month, though, they arranged another trip to London, this time to see the Indian Art exhibition at Burlington House. It was very much a demonstration to themselves that they could still organise a memorable expedition. They could pay their way too, saving up the £5 10s. that it would cost each of them, hiring a coach and staying in a hotel on the Saturday night.

Helen Sutherland wrote to Basil Grey in the Department of Oriental Antiquities at the British Museum telling him about the plans and he offered to show the Group round his Department. Arthur Whinnom

Weekend course 1948: life class

London trip 1948: the Group outside the National Gallery

drew up a schedule: overnight bus down the Great North Road, Saturday morning at the British Museum, the National Gallery ('pick a few favourite pictures to view, as time will be too short to do justice to many'), then all afternoon at the Royal Academy and an optional look at the new Institute of Contemporary Art's 'Forty Years of Modern Art'. After a night in the Imperial Hotel, Russell Square, Sunday morning was to be spent in Petticoat Lane and then at the Tate where there was a Chagall exhibition. 'These pictures may be difficult', Arthur Whinnom warned. 'Eric Newton says "Chagall's world is not easy to share."'

'5.0 pm A MEAL AND BACK—back shift?'

'It's the only way we can do it without losing time in the pits,' Whinnom told a *Journal* reporter. 'The boys put in the Friday shift and left home at 8 pm, arriving in London at 8 o'clock yesterday morning,' George Brown ('72-years-old president, ex-miner') said to Mea Allan of the *Daily Herald*, whose account of the weekend was headlined 'PIT ARTISTS GO TO TOWN From Their Slag Heap Studio'.[10]

Outside the Tate Gallery

A *News Chronicle* photographer caught them at the National Gallery, with George Brown pointing out Canada House to them, and coming down the steps of the Tate: the Group out in force, with their driver and with two or three recruits or possible recruits, among them '22-year-old miner Derek Laidlaw who is earmarked as a new member', George McLean and Fred Laidler. They were exultant, ready to face the journey home. 'I shall have to meditate on Chagall,' Arthur Whinnom was thinking. 'After I had been round his work I went to see the French Impressionists' room and was struck how insipid they seemed to be.' In the twelve years since their last visit they and the Tate had changed. Now they were beholden to no one.

'When their coach stopped at the National Gallery,' the *News Chronicle* reported, 'the miners noticed a pavement artist holding a one-man exhibition. They had a whip-round for him.'[11]

10

We've learnt from each other. One's helped another, one's criticised another without anybody being offended, which is a great thing I think. Here it's opinion without penalty.

FRED LAIDLER

In July 1948 Arthur Jeffress, of the new Hanover Gallery in Mayfair, came looking for suitable works for an exhibition of Sunday Painters he was planning for the autumn. He took seven pictures away with him, but was disappointed. They didn't conform to his idea of the properly primitive.

'I am afraid that not all of the pictures that I brought down from Ashington have found favour with my partners,' he wrote to Arthur Whinnom. 'As things stand at present only two of the seven that I brought will be included. These are *The Miner's Bath* by A. Rankin and *Pigeons* by James Floyd.

'I do hope that this will not occasion a great deal of disappointment. As you will remember, when I saw you all I did express my regret that your use of colour was so lacking in boldness. I cannot but think that brighter, bolder colours would cause quite a revolutionary improvement in your works.'[1]

Graham Sutherland, who had been the Hanover Gallery's first exhibitor a month or so before with paintings of shrivelled and aggressive forms on colourful grounds, described his friend Arthur Jeffress as 'romantic, even exotic' and he painted a portrait of him a few years later, a rakish figure, an American in Venice, posed in front of a length of the red damask he chose as wallhanging and bedspread. Hardly Ashington taste: what Jeffress had in mind was the artless bravado of a certain sort of Sunday painting; pictures, as Robert Melville said in his introduction to the 'Sunday Painters' catalogue, that 'are windows opening upon a land wonderfully clear and desirable in which *we* shall never have the opportunity of finding our bearings: but the painters themselves are lords of phantasmal estates.'

Three Ashington paintings were eventually shown: the Rankin and the Floyd and *El Garib* by Joseph Nicholson of Seaton Delaval Colliery, who had recently joined the Group after serving in the Eighth Army.[2]

El Garib was painted on a piece of kit-bag, all he had to hand off-duty in the desert. Circumstantially at least, it was Arthur Jeffress's most remarkable find.

'Thank you again,' he wrote, 'for so kindly arranging for me to see the paintings the other evening. I spoke to Graham Sutherland about you on my return just before he went off to the South of France. He is very interested in the work of the Group, though he agreed with me about the colours I think. I suggest that you write to him once again in the late autumn, and ask him if he will come up to talk to you all.'

Nothing came of this; indeed, apart from Oliver Kilbourn's *Coal Face Filler*, shown in the AIA's 'Coalminers' exhibition at their Lisle Street premises in 1950, 'Sunday Painters' was the Group's last showing in the South for some years. They turned to the Council for the Arts, Music and Drama in Northumberland – CAMDIN – for help to meet the costs of a weekend course in clay modelling with the Master of Sculpture at King's College as tutor. This was held in the hut, students being advised to 'provide their own eatables'. A painting weekend, conducted by Christopher Cornford, was arranged for September. Meanwhile, on 29 August they were invited to go to Alnwick Castle to

Outing to Alnwick, 1948

W. Crichton, *Pit Yard*, 1947

Fred Laidler, *Ventilator
Repairs*, 1948

Fred Laidler, *Unloading Timber*, c.1949

Fred Laidler, *Cartwright's Shop*, c.1949

Fred Laidler, *The Saw Sharpener*, 1948

Fred Laidler, *Open Drawer*, 1950s

OPPOSITE ABOVE Fred Laidler, *Hauler Foundations*, 1948

OPPOSITE BELOW Fred Laidler, *Shaft Repairs*, c.1950

Fred Laidler, *Dead Pony*, c.1948

Oliver Kilbourn, *Coal Face Drawers. c.*1956

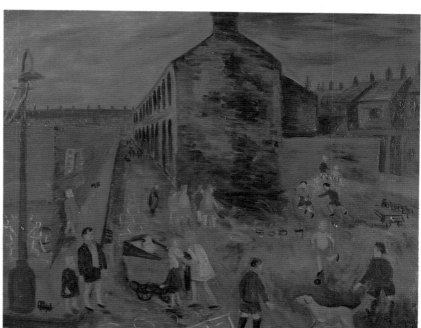

Oliver Kilbourn, *Children Playing, c.*1953

J. F. Harrison, *Band Parade*, c.1968

Jimmy Floyd, *Miner's Hobby*, 1971

Weekend course: Kilbourn, Floyd, Dobson

discuss art with the teachers' training college there. In November, as part of Ashington's effort for the United Nations Appeal for Children, they put on an exhibition which raised £25 18s.6d., an amount exceeded only by the Ashington Rotary Club and two local churches. More than half the works were landscapes. Warkworth Castle was a popular subject. Joseph Nicholson showed *Seaton Delaval Hall* and Leslie Brownrigg lent a drawing of himself by Robert Lyon.

Membership of the Group was changing. George Brownrigg had left once Robert Lyon had gone to Edinburgh. Others, like Leslie Brownrigg, Andy Foreman and Andy Rankin, did little painting. Apart from Jimmy Floyd and Oliver Kilbourn, the most productive members now were the newcomers Len Robinson and Fred Laidler.

'The first night I ever came,' Laidler remembered, 'I brought a little sketch of a castle and an old man – George Brown it would have been – who saw it criticised it most severely and when I went away they thought I wouldn't come back. But I did, and I'm pleased I did. I learnt to take criticism.'[3]

Fred Laidler had his own range of subjects. There was the occasional outside scene – *Fish and Chips* – but mostly he concentrated on his preoccupations as a colliery joiner: timber being stacked in the yard, saws being sharpened, wood-working tools, precise graining, specialised tasks. 'I think after you've been painting awhile you tend to see pictures in things that you never would have seen before.

Generally I have a good idea of what I'm going to do before I start. I think about it for quite a long time.'[4]

When he was just an apprentice Laidler saw a dead pony being brought to the surface in a tram normally used for taking pit props to the face. The image remained with him, and the knowledge that such casualties went to the knacker's yard in Bedlington.

The normality of Laidler's paintings, the lack of emotive fuss in *Ponies Going Down*, the detailed job description of 'Hauler Foundations', the difficulties of *Ventilator Repairs* where small men scramble near a blast of steam, is their strength. 'Whenever I paint a picture I always know exactly what I'm going to do. How it comes out may not be exactly the way I wanted it, but I always have a good idea of what I want.' The wheel, spokes, toolbox and hub carefully placed in the foreground of *The Cartwrights* are reminiscent of the litter of broken weapons in the National Gallery's *Rout of San Romano*. Robert Lyon would have been delighted at Laidler's implicit appreciation of Uccello's use of perspective.

'Every man paints his own type of picture and if you ask for anybody's opinion they'll give it to you. That's one thing about the art club. You paint a picture and there's something not exactly right, you come here and somebody will say well, if you had done this instead of that, that would have put it right. A lot of amateurs, they paint a picture and they think, because it's an oil painting, they think it's marvellous and they are blind to its faults.'

Tom McSloy, *Resetting Arch Girders*, 1946

Tom McSloy, *Resetting Arch Girders*, 1946

Fred Laidler was the industrious apprentice of the Group, extending the coverage of pit life into another department. In *Resetting Arch Girders*, Tommy McSloy, a blacksmith, contributed to the permanent collection a striking account of a process whereby girders bent by pressure underground were worked back into shape on a pegged steel plate. If Laidler's *Ventilator Repairs* owed something to Stanley

Stanley Spencer, *Shipbuilding on the Clyde*, 1942

Len Robinson,
Joiner's Shop,
c.1950

Len Robinson,
The Saw Pit, 1946

Spencer's *Mending Cowls, Cookham* (reproduced in Eric Newton's monograph on Spencer for *Penguin Modern Painters*), McSloy, it would appear, had been impressed by Spencer the War Artist among the rivets and templates of the Clydeside shipbuilders. Len Robinson, who worked as a builder, saw the forge at Woodhorn Colliery in a cosy light. His attitude was more quirky than McSloy's or Laidler's. He painted domestic scenes: wash-day and a bout of home decoration with the whole family pitching in. He rounded out the view of Ashington life in the post-war era, rather in the style of the old jokes page of the *Ashington Collieries Magazine* or 'Talk o' the Toon' in the *Ashington and District Advertiser*. You sense memories in the joiner's shop where he had once worked, dust in the eyes of the unfortunate down below in *The Saw Pit*, stale gossip at the Rendez-Vous Café.

While visitors to the South Bank exhibition during the Festival of Britain in 1951 could walk through a length of coal-mine made of plaster painted black, Ashington's 'stunt-packed Festival programme', lasting a week, had no appreciable educational content. 'Wansbeck', now writing the Ashington Opinion column of the *Ashington and District Advertiser*, had no time for the spoil-sports who disapproved of the contests involved. 'The public will not line the pavements in thousands or flock to a park in thousands to see local cultural groups in action, but they did turn out in large numbers to see a wheelbarrow race, a ham sandwich race and an onion eating competition, a women's football match and a street carnival.'[5]

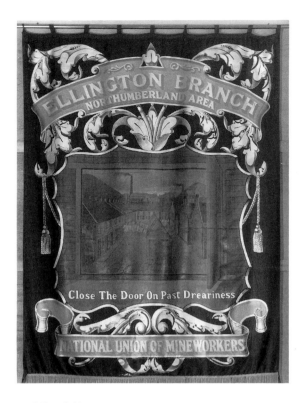

The Ellington Branch banner, designed by Oliver Kilbourn in 1951.

The following week the Northumberland miners' picnic was held at Morpeth. The Ellington contingent had a new banner to parade, designed by one of their branch members, Oliver Kilbourn. 'Close the Door on Past Dreariness' was the text, and framed in the traditional ornate scrollwork were his lofty views of pre-war housing on one side – grim, colourless, overshadowed by pitheaps – and, on the other, a clean and open-plan modern housing estate. This was to be the future, pitheaps cleared away, open drains and netties a bad memory.

The Ellington banner was designed, like all the others converging on gala day, to remind mineworkers of bygone struggles, continuing purposes and the necessary resolve. Much had been achieved in a few years, as Oliver Kilbourn acknowledged: 'After nationalisation there was more concern for the miner's welfare as regards working conditions, and methods of dust suppression and control of water were introduced. There was a free issue of protective clothing for particular jobs. Lighting was very much improved and gear such as picks, explosives and hand drills were provided free.' With Ellington Colliery expanding steadily under the sea, prosperity seemed assured as never before. 'Past dreariness', though, remained almost indistinguishable from present dreariness.

In September 1953 Norman Shrapnel visited Ashington for the *Manchester Guardian* and reported that its inhabitants had 'gone on mining into the quite exceptional virtues of their past, rich seams of enlightenment which made them pioneers in matters of welfare, pit safety, technical training and – more disinterestedly than many would think proper to-day – general education. Yet Ashington stands, in the physical sense, roughly where it did. Just as the output from its three shafts has been pretty steady for half a century, so have the dark crowded lines of its miners' cottages seen little change but extension.'[6]

Shrapnel praised the Choral and Operatic Society and regretted the passing of the *Ashington Collieries Magazine*. He described the district as 'a country both congested and spacious: there are sixty acres of playing fields around Ashington, huge rooms in some of its 22 clubs, and in the institute – provided by what is claimed to be the only self-supporting miners' welfare scheme in Britain – a main hall so vast that they used to play bowls there in winter.

'Nobody would believe – would want to believe – that it is all study and song, drama and quartets, higher thoughts and flower shows in this brave old world. What of the mighty pie-eating contests, once so famous in these parts? These seem to have died, though onion-eating championships are still talked about with a surreptitious awe.

'It is its painters, however, who have more than anybody else carried the name of Ashington over the grey mountains. Working miners are among the best painters in the Ashington Art Group which can claim to be a "school" with more truth than usual ... "It's cutting out the fripperies, getting at the essential shapes and the hard core of what the individual painter has to say," a member explained. "Right from the start we tried to spread the paint about and keep clear of the academic rules."

'The results? Hundreds of paintings are stacked in the studio hut which members bought from their sales, and the sheer liveliness of fish-and-chip shop, holiday camp, and similar uninhibited scenes nearly knocks you down ... Sometimes a member will sneak off into the country and paint a conventional landscape "for a little light relief".'

That summer members of the Group had been to see Helen Sutherland in Matterdale, above Ullswater. Winifred Nicholson had met them and Kathleen Raine had read her poetry to them. Arthur Whinnom wrote to thank their hostess. 'What a planning you must have done both for our spiritual and corporeal appetites ... How inarticulate I feel to say all I know we feel deep down about you and your goodness, I think you know though that yourself, your house and the lovely things about you are something we have enjoyed, are enriched by, and make an abiding memory ...'[7]

Joseph Nicholson's letters to Arthur Whinnom and the Group, written during his two-week journey to Seattle with wife and children at the end of 1953, had a very different tone: the emigrant's agitation overlaid with determined optimism. From the 'Britannic' in mid-Atlantic he wrote describing the comforts of the tourist class cabin, the abundance of food and cigarettes and the gap between life moving westwards and the life left behind in Seaton Delaval.

'I got checked by my wife today for making the same mistake too often. Instead of saying "Shall we go on deck dear", I have been coming out with "Wat aboot gannan ti bank lass". Mind you, I have refined a little because only this morning, without me even using any effort, I said, "Shall we go to the surface" – however she still found room to complain. I'll have to watch my step when I want to use the lavatory or I will be saying netty and folks might think I am after some of the smashing young stuff that hover around the ~~cage~~ elevator.

'There's a swimming pool but it is too cold for me. You see Delaval had no pit-head baths and I was used to pulling the bath-tin near the fire and it makes a difference you know!'[8]

After a three-and-a-half day bus ride across the States the Nicholsons were met by uncles and aunts in Seattle. It turned out that work wasn't as easy to come by as he had been led to expect. He tried selling his sketches in the big stores and there was the promise of a job later on as a draughtsman. In the meantime he settled for being a handyman for the Washington Co-op Farmers' Association. His letters were full of the luxuries Americans regarded as normal: cars, refrigerators, central heating systems and TV: 'very prominent but radio still popular'. New Year brought out the expatriate Geordie in him. 'I have many relatives here and we all congregated at one of my uncles' house and my aunt being a "lettered" pianist we were soon having the time of our lives singing Geordie songs. At midnight my uncle performed the ceremony of being First Foot and we wondered what was going to happen because we knew there was no coal (I haven't seen even a bit of duff since I left England): nevertheless Uncle wasn't going to be beat and he landed in with a plank of wood – George Brown could have made good use of it . . .

'I enjoyed your news about the Group activities and I feel I am missing quite a good deal. Yes, I am sure Oliver's lectures on Watercolours are full of useful hints and full of interest. I know that, because I had the good fortune to hear one of his addresses and, besides the knowledge I gained from his talk on the many papers and their uses, I was altogether interested in his manner of instruction. He is good, and I should know because I was a trained instructor in the R.A. during the war at Aldershot and that in itself was an achievement. I'm not trying to show myself off, only to prove that I am in a position to say that Oliver is good.'[9]

'When I was a youth I was very shy, and since I got into this Group and so-forth I've been able to express myself better,' Oliver Kilbourn said. 'I never read novels or anything like that: it didn't seem to me as if

The Journal / 7th aug. 1959.

ART IS 'THE ...AN'

25-year-old
...ke a claim

SOME of Ashington Art Group (above) give a little friendly criticism on one of their member's paintings. From left to right are: Mr. Edwin Harrison, Mr. Oliver Kilbourn, Mr. Fred Laidler, Mr. Arthur Whinnon and Mr. Walter Bell. Below, Mr. Whinnon, founder secretary of the group, at work.

they were true to life. I only went in for reading about art, and astronomy and that sort of thing.'

Looking back over the previous twenty years, Harry Wilson described in 1971 the routine of Group meetings, changed from Tuesdays to Mondays in the late Fifties to suit one of the older members. 'We have lectures occasionally, arranged by Oliver who has a camera and projector. He gets different ideas into his head, different things. For instance he got quite excited about Bewick and he did slides of that.'[10]

Over the years the slide library grew until it became a comprehensive and detailed history of art, with particular emphasis on Bewick, Breughel, Hogarth and, above all, Turner.

'The meetings are not organised in any particular way,' Harry Wilson said. 'We haven't a set arrangement. It all depends on what we're interested in at the time. In the case of, say, a painting session we decide what each person feels like painting. We don't do a great deal of painting in our studio, we do it mostly at home but we bring the pictures in for discussion and criticism and the artist says what he's aiming at and the group discusses whether they think he's achieved what he's set out to do. Otherwise very informal.'

In August 1959 they held an exhibition at the Laing. Robert Lyon came to select the pictures but didn't attend the opening. The older members, who remembered her, were amazed to see Helen Sutherland walk in, helped by a young companion. It was the last time they saw her. Reactions to this exhibition were less than enthusiastic. Scott Dobson, in the *Newcastle Evening Chronicle*, said, 'I feel that there is no doubt about the fact that the Group has lost its initial impact; things are better in Ashington today than when the Group was first formed and the protesting expressionism springing from genuine feeling has to a large extent disappeared.' Yet, he added, 'Oliver Kilbourn can still paint the soul of Ashington and I make no apology for this purple phrase. I know Ashington and I think I know a good painting when I see it. Therefore, I feel that many of his works have a validity and honesty about them that cannot be matched by the more recipe-minded professional social realist.'[11]

Scott Dobson, who was later to acquire, through a series of booklets on 'Larn Yerself Geordie' and the like, a reputation as spokesman for the region, already saw the Group as part of the past. *Coal Face Drawers*, Oliver Kilbourn's most powerful, most expressive underground painting, was precisely what Scott Dobson and, indeed, all previous admirers of the Group had always wanted to see. It is an expert's account, close-up and terse, of one of the most hazardous jobs in mining. The style, all abrupt angles and sweaty highlights, holds the tension of the moment before one more timber prop is pulled out and the roof of the exhausted working caves in with what Sid Chaplin once described as 'a wheeze and a sigh like a comfortable old giant after a meal'.[12]

Coal Face Drawers was more than a demonstration of how far the Group had come since the lumpiness of Les Brownrigg's Walpamur *Miner* twenty years before. It was Oliver Kilbourn's experiment with what he had learnt of Rubens' technique, as used by Van Gogh when he painted the peasants and miners of the Borinage. 'Usually painters work darks into lights. Well, I generally paint lights into the dark. It's a technique that you've got to be quick at, painting into wet, light into dark.'

The others painted sporadically. Len Robinson did a picture of the open-cast mine beyond Bedlington, not a promising subject but worth recording, they agreed. Jimmy Floyd painted fairgrounds and circuses, flower-pieces for his relatives, allotments and a schoolyard with two hundred children in it. Then there was Abstraction.

'I like playing about with abstract shapes myself,' said Harry Wilson. 'It's satisfying, like playing a game of draughts or chess, to shift shapes around and find where there's a nice relationship between them. I wouldn't say it's *art* though.'

'I've done a little bit of abstract painting, but whether the result is worth the bother I don't know,' Oliver Kilbourn added – he showed a number of them during the 1964 Ashington Arts Festival – and Fred Laidler tried constructing sculpture using wooden shapes from the colliery patternshop. These were exhibited, along with the Group's other recent work (Floyd's *Eisteddfod*, Jack Harrison's *Krazy Kats*) at the Bondgate Gallery in Alnwick run by George McLean, a former member whose teaching job had taken him away from Ashington. Laidler's *Construction 1*, *Construction 2* and *Construction 3* were no problem. They just stood there. Difficulties however arose with the more obviously appealing pictures, Jimmy Floyd's in particular. Whose were they, the Group's or the individual's?

Under Rule 18: Exhibition of Members' Works and Money Accruing from Sales Thereof, it had been decided, back in 1956, that Fred and Oliver were to be 'prime selectors' of works for the Permanent Collection. But when, in 1961, the possibility presented itself of paintings being sold through Scott Dobson's Westgate Gallery in Newcastle, the Group faced being weakened or compromised by those who, as Arthur Whinnom put it, wanted 'a finger in both pies – Group activities and Private Finangling'. Whinnom's death in May 1962 and George Brown's a year later, meant that the responsibility of keeping the original aims in mind now rested almost entirely upon Oliver, Harry and Fred.

This was a period of increasing celebrity for those identified with miners' art. Norman Cornish exhibited alongside L. S. Lowry at the Stone Gallery in Newcastle. Tom McGuinness, a former 'Bevin Boy'

who had attended classes at the Spennymoor Settlement became well-known, and heading the professionals, there was Josef Herman, to whom the miners of Ystradgynlais in South Wales were beings from a simplified world, a 'mixture of sadness and grandeur'.

Fred Laidler's reliefs hung on the walls of the hut, boxed and alien, echoing movements that bore no relation to life in Ashington. They had the virtue, though, of being experiments that invited no sentimental associations. They showed that the Group would not, after all, join the socialworkers-realists, the semi-professionals, the School of Lowry.

The most colourful of these, the Gulley Jimson of coalminer painters, was Clancy Sigal's more or less fictitious Davie, hero of *Weekend in Dinlock*, a documentary novel about life and creative struggle in the Yorkshire coalfield, published in 1960. Davie is 'a man who piles it on and piles it on,' torn between art and the pit, art and domesticity. '"Ah don't paint fancy lahk they do in London. Ah paint the truth Ah know."'[13]

Davie thinks of turning professional yet 'that old dread returns, the possibility that he can only produce his paintings as an act of escape. Dinlock is his shroud, but it may also be his motor, charging him up with a creative desperation which sends him to the easel as the only way to mark himself live.' Sigal witnesses the agonising. Davie he knows felt 'inferior but also a little proud of his art' when he spent weekends in London, yet also 'proud of his class and of the one thing nobody could take away from him, the fact that he was a miner, a Yorkshire miner, a village miner, and the very cream at that, a collier on the coal face'. That settles it. Davie remains a miner. One suspects that his were the paintings Arthur Jeffress had hoped to discover on his trip North.

II

A funny thing, once you've painted a picture you feel it's part of your life, you know.

OLIVER KILBOURN

On the evening of 22 January 1971 the Laing Art Gallery held a private view of an Arts Council exhibition 'The Helen Sutherland Collection of Modern Art', described by Nicolete Gray in her introduction to the catalogue as 'an historic record of the period in English art from 1925 to 1945'. Helen Sutherland had died in 1965.[1]

I was living in Newcastle, teaching at the Royal Grammar School, and went along to the Laing that Friday night in my capacity as art critic of the *Newcastle Journal*. I had already seen the exhibition a month before in London, at the Hayward Gallery. The touring version didn't include the Mondrian that once hung above the stairs at Rock Hall. In its absence the Ben Nicholsons stood out. There were dozens of them along one wall, jugs blending into sparse landscapes and terrain giving way to white reliefs. At this point George McLean from Alnwick stopped me and took me over to a group of four or five elderly men, well wrapped up, standing apart from the crowd of Friends of the Laing chattering over their wine and twiglets. They were the Ashington Group.

Though I had heard of them and had seen some of Helen Sutherland's examples of their work down in London, I had assumed that the Group was as wholly Thirties as Unit One or the GPO Film Unit. But with a vigour quite out of keeping with Laing occasions they put me right, going through what they had done, what they aimed for, recalling Helen Sutherland and discussing Ben Nicholson's eye for pattern, the evasiveness of David Jones and the qualities of George Blessed's *Pit Scene*. I was welcome to come over to Ashington and see what they had there. Why not Monday, 8 o'clock? One of them, bulky and short of breath, with heavy glasses, drew me a map on the back of the Private View card. Down Central Woodhorn Road, on the left just beyond the Central Hall and Co-Op, follow the link fencing and it was next to the Veterans. The name was over the door.

I had little trouble finding the hut, despite the fog. The door opened and inside there was a crush of overcoats and mufflers, eight people at least, feet stamping, arms clapped together as the fire was lit. Then the paintings were produced from all corners, some recent and garish, some so faint and grubby they had to be rubbed with a sleeve and even then remained dim. 'Aye, that's the Deputy's kist – chest – and the Deputy's sitting with his elbow on his kist and the other fellas have arrived and they sat down generally and had a smoke before they were detailed off to the various places.' 'You see in those days you were allowed to smoke.'

Paintings emerged from under tables and from behind seats, paintings of fairs, markets, streets, leek-growers. 'They have their own particular way of feeding the leeks, shredded leather and bottled beer. The beard's carefully washed and combed and then all the leaves are done with milk.' A picture of a bowler in a flat cap with a calculating smile. 'This is a local character, lived at North Seaton wasn't it? He was a regular attender at the bowling green. Pile they called him: Harry Pile.'

Harry Wilson was the readiest with explanations. Oliver Kilbourn, quietspoken but persistent, kept pointing out significant aspects. 'It's a family shifting. They just had to put their things in the street, load them onto the flat cart and go away. Everybody saw what you did, but that

TOP: Harry Wilson and Jimmy Floyd, 1971
BOTTOM: Oliver Kilbourn and Fred Laidler, 1971

Len Robinson, *The Bowler*, 1950s

[158]

didn't really matter because people were always going in and out of each other's houses. You couldn't hide anything from anybody.' Fred Laidler produced his painting of a tool drawer with the wood-graining and dove-tails demonstrably accurate. 'One time I used to paint drab sort of pictures,' said Jimmy Floyd. 'But now I like a bit of colour in them.' He brought out a merry-go-round, done in enamel paints.

There were ten members active in the Group. Yet, as the pictures piled up, I could see that this, the Permanent Collection, was the Group's hoard and that the hut was what had kept the Group going beyond its heyday. It would have been easy to see it all as a sort of archive, a small, local episode preserved. But there were too many ideas, too many lively interests, still engaged there. What had once been a formal WEA class was obviously now a proud stronghold, first and last of its kind. An inscription over the fireplace said as much. By the time I left the fog had turned snowy and Ashington was dead quiet.

In a letter to Robert Lyon, now retired from Edinburgh and living in Eastbourne, Jimmy Floyd referred to me saying 'we have become good friends, he is like one of us in the Group'. A few months later, in the summer, we spent five days with Tristram Powell and a BBC crew filming an account of the Group through the eyes of the three surviving founder members, Jimmy Floyd, Oliver Kilbourn and Harry Wilson. Most of the time was spent in the hut going through the works, discussing the sculptures and the guiding principles. 'I can't say I've ever enjoyed the experience of painting or drawing like one would experience a good golf swing or something like that,' Harry Wilson said. 'It's always been much more serious and concentrated.'[2] I asked Oliver Kilbourn what advice he would give to people who wanted to do as they had done. 'Well, I would suggest they try the same thing that we did: try and paint a picture of their very own, the picture that nobody else has painted before, copied off nobody; something you feel strongly about. That's what I'd say: start painting. It's as simple as that.'

We went out one afternoon to some allotments and talked about pigeons ('The ring's put on when they are about five days old, you see, and it never comes off,') and leek-growing. 'These leeks are bred and bred again many times over by the men themselves. The seed isn't bought, it's selected by them and this has gone on from generation to generation.'

At Ashington Colliery we stood on a gantry and Oliver Kilbourn pointed out the brickyard where he had started work at thirteen. 'I was there only about a year and I went down the pit, the second shaft, the middle one, when I was fourteen.' Going down, he remembered, 'you used to get that sinking feeling in the pit of your stomach till you got half-way down and then you seemed to feel as if you were riding out of it, coming upwards instead of going down.'

Photographs of Ashington by Sirkka-Liisa Konttinen, 1971

They talked about the different pits, the open-cast workings over at Bedlington, already being landscaped into a golf course, and about Ellington Colliery stretching five miles under the sea while at the other end of the seam 'the coal comes to bank just alongside of the colliery. Men used to come and take it out of the pits in the fields. That's where you get the story about butterflies. There were butterflies in the pits.'

At Rock Hall, which had become a Youth Hostel, they sat in the garden and reminisced. Harry Wilson: 'How long is it since we were here? Thirty years, maybe twenty-five, and a lot of things have happened since that, including I've got a lot older and a lot more feeble than I was then and with fewer enthusiasms. But this is important to me. The days that I spent here and places like this are what seem to me worthwhile in the life that I've had.'

'Well, I thought coming back here would hit me hard,' said Oliver Kilbourn. 'Actually it's overwhelmed us in a way, but a subdued way. After a bit I begin to feel it coming towards me: I can feel a little bit of the passion of the past.'

The film was shown the following January, three days before the opening, at the DLI Museum in Durham, of an exhibition of the Group's work. 'We (the lads) were told it's the best exhibition they have ever put on show,' Jimmy Floyd wrote to Robert Lyon. 'As I have always been, if possible, in the background I did feel ever so pleased.'[3] A month later, on 20 February, Harry Wilson died.

Later that year the exhibition went to Sunderland, Sheffield, Manchester and Cardiff before being finally shown at the Whitechapel Art Gallery in April 1973 where it was the accompaniment to Claude Rogers' retrospective, a thorough statement of Euston Road School loyalties. 'There is more in common than you might expect between these two shows,' Margaret Richards wrote in *Tribune*. 'Downstairs the highly professional professor, upstairs the non-professional miner artists. "Paint what you see" and "Paint what you know" are facets of a similar untrendy commitment to reality. These artists all paint with single-minded provincial integrity, as if Picasso had never existed.'[4]

Len Robinson, Oliver Kilbourn and Fred Laidler in the Hut, 1971

Travelling exhibitions reintroduced the aims and achievements of the Group but they were no solution to the problem of finding an appropriate home for the permanent collection. As Guy Brett said in *The Times*: 'In our museums you find the works of one or two favoured naïve painters – a Lowry, an Alfred Wallis. But it would be a great mistake to isolate one or two pictures by the Ashington painters and put them in a museum on aesthetic grounds, because their strength is that together they tell a vivid story.'[5]

A temporary solution was to take up an offer of help from the National Coal Board. 'We are very keen to see that the Group's work is suitably housed, as it so clearly deserves to be,' the NCB Chairman, Sir Derek Ezra, wrote.[6] It was arranged that the paintings would be transferred for safekeeping to the NCB staff training centre at Long Benton on the outskirts of Newcastle, the idea being to open the area where the paintings hung – in common rooms and on the main stairs – one day a week to the public. 'You wouldn't recognise the old Art Group hut now as all the pictures have gone and the place looks very bare,' Oliver wrote to me in September 1975. 'It was a bit of a wrench parting with them, but of course it is for the best.'[7]

He and his wife Peggy, who had recently retired from her job as librarian at Ashington Branch Library, were flown to Berlin by the NCB in February 1977 for the opening of *Englische Arbeiterkunst*, an exhibition, organised by the Neue Gesellschaft für bildende Kunst, which consisted almost entirely of Ashington paintings.[8]. Jimmy Floyd had died the year before and Oliver Kilbourn was now called on as the surviving founder member to speak for what *The Times*'s obituary for Robert Lyon, in June 1978, described as 'a significant early venture in helping working men to articulate their feeling through paint'. In August 1978 the Kilbourns went to Rotterdam for the start of a twelve-month tour of fifty of the paintings ('Engelse mijnwerkerskunst') in the Netherlands.[9]

The following year the Ashington Group took its place in 'Thirties', an encyclopaedic Arts Council exhibition at the Hayward which I co-organised.[10] The section was called 'Society Observed', a theme stretching from the AIA to the Euston Road School, taking in a Lowry,

ENGLISCHE
ARBEITERKUN

a Percy Horton (*Unemployed Man*), stills from *Spare Time* and *Coalface*, 'Worktown' photographs by Humphrey Spender, photographs of village colleges, pithead baths and the Peckham Health Centre, a Julian Trevelyan pit village collage and his photo of the Group at work in the YMCA hut. The six Ashington pictures, surrounding an autographed copy of the Unprofessional Painting catalogue, included Harry Wilson's *10 am*, Oliver Kilbourn's *Sunday Dinner*, Jimmy Floyd's *Snow Scene* (the allotments near Woodhorn Colliery) and William Scott's banner-bold *Bedlington Terrier*. It all fitted together, the professional and the unprofessional, the ideal, the factual and the exemplary.

This could have been the end of the 'Experiment in Art Appreciation', neatly slotted into socio-art history. But no: the Group, in the person of Oliver Kilbourn, still had work to do. The Durham exhibition, seven years before, had set him thinking that he should attempt a full and complete record, a visual memoir, of his experiences, starting as a pom-pom boy on the compressed air coal-cutting machines in 1917, going on to be a putter-lad, a coal face drawer, a salvage drawer and a wasteman. The 'Boy's Day' and pen and wash 'Pit Scenes' of 1939–40 were the basis of the scheme but as he developed it, using acrylics on paper, the memories were directed into detailed narrative. 'My Life as a Pitman' became an exhibition,[11] arranged by Lynda Morris at the Midland Group in Nottingham in 1977 and a year later at the Artists' Market, a gallery in Covent Garden run on co-operative lines by Vera Russell, where in 1976 a selection of affirmative peasant paintings from Hu county, Shansi province, in Cultural Revolutionary China had been shown. Though more subdued in tone, 'My Life as a Pitman' was taken to be a North Country counterpart to the colourful rural Chinese scenes.[12]

There is no exaggeration, though, in the Kilbourn paintings. We are guided through the workings, peering this way and that, our eyes getting used to the darkness. We learn more about the artist as we proceed.

'Some people write their memoirs when they retire, but because I am a poor writer and a much better artist I decided to paint my memoirs as a pitman.'

'I wouldn't say I had a driving ambition to get down the pit. I just stayed down there fifty years – a working life. After a lot of groaning and grumbling you took a pride in your job you know. It's a very skilful job.'

The business of drilling a shot and firing it, the art of hewing, the effort of feeding the conveyer, then shifting the belt onto a new track and filling off a face: every procedure is illustrated with loving care. There are three pictures of how to manoeuvre a chummin (empty tub) near the face. 'Why do three? It was to show that it wasn't just a simple action. That the putter lad had to get the tub in, turn it round and then shove it in from behind – like a matador with a bull: twist and let it go. Awkward to do but graceful, like a dance step 1 2 3. Quite unique I think.'[13]

Looking back Kilbourn saw his fourteen-year-old self, remote now as though at the far end of a peepshow, clearing a fresh cut in the coalface, dragging a compressed air hose along to the main supply pipe and then, on his own, fastening full tubs onto the trot (endless rope) that led out to the shaft and brought empty tubs in return.

'I remember after all these years the bond of friendship I had with many of the ponies. When one went into the stables at the beginning of the shift to collect your pony the first thing he did was to neigh and shove his muzzle into you as you patted his neck and belly and said hello Clem, Dandy, Moss, Spot or whatever he was called, "What fettle the Day", then a vibrating purr emanated from him with a stamping of feet, and after letting him have a drink at the trough, you were all set for the day.'

There are thirty-eight paintings in 'My Life as a Pitman' and they were followed by others dealing with further aspects of work and leisure ('what I did between shifts') as they occurred to him. They run uninterrupted, nothing omitted except what he regarded as so personal as to be untypical.

'Unfortunately, when I was about eleven, my father had an accident in the pit and damaged his back. He was brought home on a flat cart and never worked again. There was just a little bit of compensation, not much like, but it helped. Once I'd left school I became the breadwinner more or less, maintaining the whole family on fourteen shillings a week till my sisters got jobs.'[14]

'I was a damn good miner, though I say it myself. I was strong and I liked the life. You are battling against nature. Not just this nature all around but what was laid down millions of years ago. That was the life I painted.'[15]

Oliver Kilbourn, 'My Life as a Pitman' (*The Deputy's Kist*), 1976

12

This exhibition is another demonstration of friendly activities between the Chinese and British governments and peoples. It will help us to know the artistic ability and achievements of the British miners.

ZHOU ERFU Vice-Minister of Culture, Chinese People's Republic, April 1980

In the summer of 1979 an invitation was extended by the Chinese Ministry of Culture, through the Chinese People's Association for Friendship with Foreign Countries and the Society for Anglo-Chinese Understanding, to the Ashington Group: the BBC film had been seen some years before, and the time was right, three years after the death of Chairman Mao, for the Chinese people to see something of what worker artists in another country had accomplished. The British Council was persuaded that this would be a good opportunity to re-establish 'co-operation in the field of cultural exchange', as Counsellor T. J. B. George of the British Embassy in Peking put it. So, in April 1980 I, together with Peter Thiele of SACU and Andrea Rose of the British Council, took the pick of the permanent collection to China. Shortly before, on 28 March, a reception was held at the Chinese Embassy in Portland Place for the Group. It was their last collective trip to London and Jack Harrison, the Kilbourns and the Laidlers, far outnumbered by NCB and Embassy officials, found the occasion sticky, the buffet dinner in particular hard to take. Arthur Whinnom's words, long ago, when he had talked of 'an affinity between the people who created those studies we looked upon and ourselves'[1] would have served well as a vote of thanks over the glazed prawns and hundred-year-old eggs. 'Nothing suggests a tortuous mentality but rather, a lofty, poetic yet simple expression . . . We are happy in having had the privilege of direct contact with the glory of Chinese Art.'

A month later in the Peking Art Gallery, the time came to open the British Council crates. One by one the pictures were lifted out and unwrapped: Les Brownrigg's *Miner*, impassively shovelling; Jimmy Floyd's *Miner*, seated in full kit, having a last smoke before the descent; Arthur Whinnom's *Pit Incident*. Some of the titles caused trouble.

Opening the Ashington crates in Peking, 1980

Clocking In? Bait Time? Pigeon Crees almost defeated the translator. Eventually she understood them to be 'Dove Dwellings'.

Helpers with bamboo poles hooked the paintings high on the walls. This, they said, was necessary in order that the masses, standing four or five deep, could get a good look. Polite efficiency gave way to smiles and enthusiasm as they began pointing out details to each other: universal behaviour. The slyness of domino players, the soulfulness of the singer in *Saturday Night at the Club*, the children getting underfoot in *Spring Fever*. But *Progging the Mat*? What could that be, asked the translator, abandoning her Standard English dictionary. Rag rug-making methods were explained. *Fish and Chips* then? That was easy: 'Traditional English Fare'.

After the opening ceremony[2] there were meetings with artists, professional and unprofessional, lectures to give and visits to the places where the exhibition was to go in the course of the next few months, all of them mining centres: Datong and Taiyuan in Shansi province, Fushun and Shenyang, formerly Mukden, in Liaoning province, formerly Manchuria. In discussion after discussion the same questions cropped up. How representative were these paintings? How did they compare with traditional art in the West? Why were such paintings no longer being produced by the Ashington miners? What did the Ashington miners think of abstract art?

The Ashington Group, I suggested, was a shining example of art for art's sake combined with art for social ends and art as a means of self-discovery and self-help. The Group, I added, went through an

[166]

abstract phase in the Fifties, for it had been determined to explore every possibility. The Group could serve as a model for others.

It turned out that the peasant painters of Hu county were no longer to be regarded as admirable. Exhortations to 'Learn from Huxian' had ceased and the paintings had gone out of circulation, discredited partly because they were identified with the Great Leap Forward of 1958 and what had followed, and partly because of the way their reputation had been shaped by the cultural cadres. China was in an uncertain state, just beginning to open up. Professional artists especially were either tainted by the recent past or re-emerging, still dazed and wary. Within a couple of years exhibitions of Western art – German Expressionist woodcuts, French Impressionists, even American Abstract Expressionists – were to fill the programme of the Peking Art Gallery. But in 1980 extreme caution prevailed. The Ashington Group represented both reassurance (that the unprofessional could be considered as exponents of a particular, populist sort of art) and that more difficult, more revealing genre: art as history.[3]

The Huxian painters – there were more than a thousand of them, it was said, by 1976 – may have enrolled in art classes at the behest of the

中英美术交流的一朵新花

——《英国矿工画展览》观后

　　春暖花开，《英国矿工画展览》在中国美术馆开幕了。这是中英两国人民友好往来的新见证，是中英美术交流的一朵新花。
　　画展展出了英国阿欣顿矿区十四位工人业余画家的五十一幅作品。这些作品大部分创作于一九三五——一九五五年之间。它们不仅在一定程度上生动地反映了二次世界大战前后二十年间阿欣顿矿区生活的历史面貌，工人的艰苦劳动和他们对于生活的观点和感情，而且也显示了英国工人的应受称赞的艺术创造才能和值得借鉴的艺术经验。
　　吉米·佛洛依德的《安全帽》（油画），通过描绘一个头戴安全帽、利用短暂的井上休息时间吸烟斗的矿工，表现了矿井劳动的紧张。矿工的形象很有个性，朴实动人。设色用薄涂法，暗而透明，只有在小块亮部才调和一点白色，可以看出作者对于油画方法的一定理解和掌握。在表现方法上和上述一画形成鲜明对比的是基尔伯恩的《在低矮的坑道里撑柱子》。在这幅水彩画中，作者用粗犷的笔法，概括而具有动势的形体，塑造了一个正在撑柱子的矿工形象，既表现了坑道劳动的艰苦，又表现了作为社会物质财富生产者的工人的力量。可以说是一幅具有象征意义的有力之作。
　　基尔伯恩从十三岁时起，就在煤矿做工，对童工的痛苦有深切的体会。他的组画《童工的一天》就是表现这一主题的。佛洛依德的《童工的头一项工作》、温诺姆的《发薪的日子》也从不同的角度反映了童工的生活。在《发薪的日子》一画上，发薪者的肥胖和窗外童工的瘦小形成发人深思的对比。佛·莱德勒的《新的小马下井》和《死去的小马》两画，表现了对小马的同情，又使人联想到矿工、童工的命运。
　　单从题目看，基尔伯恩的《布鲁斯大夫画像》（油画），应该是一幅肖像画，但是，作者并没有直接画布鲁斯大夫的相貌，却采取了不受时间—空间限制的构图方法，把布鲁斯大夫从事工作活动的不同场合组织到一个画面上。画面中心部位是他的诊室写字台、药品架和医疗器械以及讲授急救课的黑板。从画面四角上，则可以看到，无论刮风、下雨、雪天和黑夜，他的自行车都随时出现在病人的家门口。虽说画面上没有布鲁斯大夫的身影，可是，热心的布鲁斯大夫为了给矿工治病而日夜奔忙的形象却跃然活现在观者的心目中。这是一幅没有人物出场的肖像画。利用人物的生活环境和用具揭示人物的性格，这是西欧肖像画艺术中常取的办法，把属于不同的时间和空间的场景组织到一个画面上，则是中国绘画善用的构图。基尔伯恩把二者结合起来加以运用，取得了成功。
　　总之，具有浓厚的生活气息，以其朴实的感情动人，是英国矿工画家作品的共同特点。他们作画从自己所熟悉的生活出发，从表达对于生活的真情实感出发，从内容出发，不孤立地讲求形式和技术，没有框框套套。每幅画各有其特定的内容，因而也各有其不同的面貌。《英国矿工画展览》为我国专业和业余画家提供了很好的学习机会。我们表示祝贺展出的成功并祝愿中英两国人民之间的艺术交流不断加强和发展。　　　　　常又明

　　更正：昨日本报第四版照片说明中的"（右）"应为"（左）"，"新华社记者摄（传真照片）"，应为"南斯拉夫通讯社传真照片（新华社发）"。

The *Peking Daily* reports the opening of the Ashington exhibition

local Party branch to be schooled as commune propagandists but their busy depictions of collectivised activities, the hoeing and harvesting, scenes of electrification and the spread of literacy, were undoubtedly popular. They showed what could be, in the best of all possible communes, the successful outcome of every concerted effort, plans accomplished, quotas exceeded.

To this extent they were fulfilling orders. Artists were attached to work units, painting posters, producing woodcuts and other graphics as needed. Distinctions between those formally trained and those like Li Feng-lan, the Huxian mother of four who 'worked in the fields most of the year and had family duties at home' were, for a while, suppressed. There was no exclusivity, no superior aesthetic, for to be identified as an artist-intellectual at the time of the Great Proletarian Cultural Revolution was to be exposed to 'correction'. Only the acceptably stereotypical could serve.

It was not until around 1982 that art colleges and art magazines were revived and encouraged to develop a certain amount of stylistic diversity. By then the Huxian painters and others like them were relegated to the role of folk artists: naïves with Friendship Store potential. At Fushun in Liaoning province, in 1980, the main product of the art factory situated near the 'Sea of Coal', a vast open-cast mine, was coal-carvings. Skilled hands fashioned birds, heroic groups, smiling emblematic figures, using only anthracite, the hardest coal, achieving high polish and good-value detail. In the context of Fushun art for export – mainly for yen – the Ashington Group paintings must have seemed extraordinarily uncommercial. Hung in rooms normally used for table tennis and calligraphy displays, they were seen by thousands, shuffling past. Pigeon fanciers, whippet trainers and the like were viewed with curiosity if not incomprehension. Only the mining practices were readily understandable, it appeared. The real aims of the Group, beyond any WEA syllabus or cultural imperative, were lost on them.

In 1980 Woodhorn Colliery closed and production finished at Lynemouth, though the washer and coal preparation plant was kept going to process coal from Ellington and open-cast sites. The waste, dumped into the sea, provided a scratch living for growing numbers of seacoalers, many of them ex-miners. Chris Killip, one of a new generation of documentary photographers, saw on Lynemouth beach scenes that took one back fifty years: men scrabbling for the black gravel washed up by every tide; images of struggle in tearing wind and failing light; families encamped on the dunes in shacks and trailers, like the dustbowl refugees photographed in the days of the Great Depression.

The landmarks disappeared. Three million pounds was spent eliminating the waste heaps of Ashington and Woodhorn Collieries and

Chris Killip, *Seacoalers*, 1983

landscaping the site into the Silver Jubilee Park, declared open by the Queen Mother in April 1979.[4] Another landmark, the Alcan smelter at Lynemouth, so huge and new in Jimmy Floyd's last allotment painting, *Miner's Hobby* of 1971, went out of commission because of falling demand for aluminium during the Seventies recession. As pits closed throughout the North East, the North of England Open Air Museum, at Beamish in County Durham, expanded to feature a pithead, an underground roadway complete with simulated workings and a row of original pit cottages from Hetton le Hole. 'Something here to interest the whole family!' a Northumbria's Heritage brochure advised: 'Go down a "drift" mine and see how coal was worked, smell the home baked bread in one of the pitmen's cottages, see the animals at Home Farm.' There were plans too for turning the Woodhorn Colliery buildings into Ashington's own mining museum. An old winding wheel was unveiled by the Queen Mother in Silver Jubilee Park. 'A symbol of the community's past . . . become a signpost to its future', it was locked, for safety, and mounted on a plinth.

In August 1982 Oliver Kilbourn was informed by the Coal Board Estate Management in Gateshead that the ground rent for the hut was to be increased from an uneconomical fifty pence a year to £14. That plus the £7 quarterly standing charge for electricity seemed too much, so he was forced to a decision. For some time only he and Jack Harrison had been going to the hut on Monday nights, often alone, hoping someone else might turn up. Though the hut was getting decrepit it could have been sold but he disliked the idea of it being used for any other purpose. 'It was too precious.'[5] A contractor he approached quoted him £450 for the demolition. The Coal Board officials at Long Benton, however, arranged for the Works Department at Ashington to come and do it for nothing. Tables he gave to the Boy Scouts and the chairs went to the Veterans' next door. The rest of the furniture was sawn up and taken in his nephew's van to the council tip. Finally, in October 1983, the hut was pulled down. Within a year the site was a mass of weeds with willow herb growing through the remains of the foundations.

The miners' strike of 1984 was well-supported in Ashington. 'No need for pickets here,' the Kilbourns wrote. During the 1974 strike Fred Laidler had been so impressed by the sight of a picket remaining on duty throughout a bitterly cold night, huddled round a brazier in the snow, he had considered making it the subject of a picture, harking back perhaps to George Brownrigg's *Dawn*. But that was as far as he went. The urge to bear witness, to paint for the record, had faded. Ten years later it had gone. Throughout 1984 and into 1985 the show-down between the NUM and the Coal Board (to be renamed, in the

Ellington miners returning to work, March 1985

interests of denationalisation possibly, British Coal) dragged on. When it was over, the Ellington miners brought out their new banner – still with the Kilbourn design – to make the return to work a show of dignity, a parade almost.[6]

In March 1986 the WEA Wansbeck branch organised a fortnight of events to mark the first anniversary of the end of the strike. These included, at the Ashington Resource Centre in Council Road, an exhibition of the Group's collection, staged in the hopes of rekindling the habit of what were now termed 'community initiatives'. There were unexpected reactions. 'Some people were saying the paintings were cruel and brutal,' Anne Spendiff, an Education Worker with the Unemployed in Wansbeck, reported. WEA effort, more assertive now than at any time since the war, was directed into developing the political skills of organising tenants' groups and negotiating with the authorities. Art was taken care of in the local High Schools; art was hardly any use, it seemed. There was far more demand for Creative Writing courses. So the Ashington Group came to be regarded as a subject for research, part of a vanished culture; though the WEA conceded that, should an inspiring tutor come along, then there would be the possibility of an Ashington renaissance.

Unemployment in the area rose to twenty percent, in some places as high as thirty percent. At the beginning of 1988 it was announced that Ashington Colliery was to close, there being 'no point', British Coal said, 'in continuing further exploratory development'. This meant Ellington alone was left, the last pit in Northumberland. The future was now largely a matter of community programmes, 'retraining', early retirement, work on the allotments or the £13 overnight bus to some sort of job in London.

Plans went ahead for the Woodhorn Colliery Museum. It seemed fitting that the Ashington Group paintings should be permanently housed there, in their own gallery, not to become part of the congealed past but to remain an inspiration.

While he was still working on his 'memoirs as a pitman', Oliver Kilbourn wrote to me about the art he most admired, why he was painting and what it meant to him. 'Constable said the River Stour and Dedham Vale made him a painter of natural landscape. Alas my River Stours and Dedham Vales were in the underworld of Ashington, and I hope by staying at home like Constable that Ashington has made me as good a painter of underground pit work. After all the Egyptians didn't do so badly with the depiction of their underworld.'[7]

Art, the Ashington Group found, isn't an exclusive cult, someone else's possession, and love of art isn't escapism or false religion. It's the ability to identify, the ability to see. After the coal has been mined, all the pitheaps have been flattened and the whole purpose of Ashington has gone, their unprofessional paintings will still survive.

Acknowledgements

I wish to thank George Stephenson of the Mid Northumberland Arts Group for suggesting that I write this book, for his keen interest in seeing it completed, and for his compelling arguments for this paperback edition. Northern Arts awarded me a grant towards research costs, for which I am grateful. Mabel Lyon generously allowed me to borrow her late husband's thesis for over a year and to quote from it. To her, and her son Peter, who showed me the Ashington paintings in his possession, I owe thanks. The late Julian Trevelyan answered my questions over the years and Humphrey Spender went to great effort to secure prints from negatives thought unusable. He and Janet Adam Smith were of great help.

I also wish to thank Nicolete Gray, Nerys Johnson of the DLI Museum Durham, Sirkka-Liisa Konttinen, Hilary Laurie, Tristram Powell, Andrea Rose, Anita Smith, Anne Spendiff, Michael Standen, Nick Stanley, Humphrey Stone, who designed the book, and Dorothy Wainwright of the Mass Observation Archive at the University of Sussex.

My chief thanks go to the members of the Ashington Group, in particular those I knew (Jimmy Floyd, Len Robinson, Fred Laidler and Harry Wilson), to the surviving members, Jack Harrison and, most of all, Oliver and Peggy Kilbourn whose help and advice have been invaluable.

Illustrations acknowledgements
Works by the Ashington Group are the property of the Group except where noted below:

Black and white photographs
Stan Gamester 170, Imperial War Museum 147, Chris Killip 169, Sirkka-Liisa Konttinen 54, 159, 160, 162, National Film Archive 73, 86, 88, the late Edwin Smith 70, 71, Humphrey Spender 80, 89, Tate Gallery 30, the late Julian Trevelyan 75, 81, Henry Moore Foundation 113, Private Collections 23, 27, 33, 41, 68, 75, 85, 94, 95. Whereabouts unknown 12, 13, 26, 42, 111, 112, 114, 118, 121. Additional photography by Alex Saunderson.

Colour plates
Laing Art Gallery, Newcastle: pages 37 (top), 38 (bottom). Private collections: pages 33, 39 (bottom), 40, 57 (below), 64 (bottom), 97 (top), 101 (below right), 102 (top), 144 (bottom).

Notes

CHAPTER I

[1] Jan Gordon, *A Stepladder to Painting* (London, 1934), pp259–60.
[2] 'The Miner Artists of Ashington', *Everybody's*, 5 September 1942, p5.
[3] Robert Lyon, thesis, 'The Appreciation of Art through the Visual and Practical Approach' (Newcastle, 1942), pp57–8.
[4] Ibid., p3.
[5] Interview with the author, August 1971.
[6] WEA brochure, c.1930.
[7] Interview with the author, 1971.

CHAPTER 2

[1] Interview with the author, 1971.
[2] Robert Lyon, 'An Approach to Art', *The Highway*, December 1935.
[3] Robert Lyon, 'An Experiment in Art Appreciation', *The Listener*, 29 May 1935.
[4] Ibid.
[5] Lyon, thesis, op. cit., pp7–12.
[6] Robert Lyon, 'An Adventure in Art', *Mine*, February 1936.
[7] Quoted in Lyon, 'Art and the Ashington Miners', 'London Calling', 28 January 1945.

CHAPTER 3

[1] Interview with the author, 1971.
[2] See Nicolete Gray (Introduction), 'Helen Sutherland Collection' (Arts Council, 1970).
[3] Interview with the author, 1971.
[4] 'Ashington WEA Art Class – Visit to London', 1936.
[5] *The Listener*, 22 January 1936.
[6] Interview with the author, 1971.

CHAPTER 4

[1] Herbert Read, 'Writing into Pattern', *The Listener*, 12 June 1935.
[2] 'L.A.R.' (Robert Lyon), Catalogue introduction (Hatton Gallery, 1936).
[3] Kenneth Clark, Introduction to *Art and the Child* (London, 1948), p10.
[4] Letter to the author, October 1987.
[5] 'L.A.R.' (Robert Lyon), Catalogue introduction (Laing Art Gallery, 1938).
[6] Interview with the author, 1971.
[7] Edwin Muir reviewing *The Stars Look Down* in *The Listener*, 10 April 1935.
[8] J. B. Priestley, *English Journey* (London, 1934), p322.
[9] Clive Bell, *Civilization* (London, 1928), p256.
[10] *The Highway*, December 1935, pp44, 49.
[11] W. E. Williams, 'Art for the People', *The Listener*, 19 May 1937.
[12] R. S. Lambert (ed.), *Art in England* (Harmondsworth, 1938).

CHAPTER 5

[1] Interview with the author, 1971.
[2] George Brown, 'Art Through the Ages', *Ashington Collieries Magazine*, November 1937.
[3] Oliver Kilbourn, 'An Approach to Modern Art', *Ashington Collieries Magazine*, October 1937.
[4] Henry P. Wilson, 'Sculpture', *Ashington Collieries Magazine*, April 1937.
[5] Lyon, thesis, op. cit., pp111–12.
[6] Interview with the author, 1971.
[7] Raymond Mortimer, *New Statesman*, 17 April 1937.
[8] *Time & Tide*, 24 April 1937.
[9] *The Spectator*, 30 April 1937.
[10] See L. Morris and R. Radford, *AIA: The Story of the Artists' International Association* (Museum of Modern Art, Oxford, 1983).
[11] *The Listener*, 28 April 1937.
[12] September 1937.
[13] 'Experiment in Art Appreciation', *The Listener*, 23 March 1938.
[14] Interview with the author, 1971. The painting has been missing since 1973.
[15] Her photographs were published in 'Tyneside', *The Geographic Magazine*, November 1937.
[16] See Arthur Gordon, thesis, 'The Economic and Social Development of Ashington' (University of Newcastle, 1954).

CHAPTER 6

[1] Letter dated 27 April 1938, Lyon to Harrisson, Mass Observation Archive. Quoted in 'The Extra Dimension', thesis on MO by Nick Stanley (Birmingham, 1981).
[2] 'Unprofessional Painting', catalogue (Gateshead, 1938), p1.
[3] Julian Trevelyan, *Indigo Days* (London, 1957), ch. 5.
[4] *Living Among Cannibals* (London, 1943), p29.
[5] Quoted in James R. Spencer, 'The Northern Pageant', *Sunday Sun* (Newcastle), 25 September 1938.
[6] *Savage Civilisation* (London, 1937), p22.
[7] *English Journey*, op. cit., pp304–5.
[8] D. R. O. Thomas to Arthur Whinnom, 3 October 1938. Group Archive.
[9] *Sunday Sun*, 25 September 1938.
[10] *Savage Civilisation*, op. cit., p360: 'In the New Hebrides *every* man is a simple material artist with keynote efficiency; art is from *ars* – skill; art is practical skill guided by rules . . . individual creative art would be against the whole training of native life.'
[11] See also L. Adam, *Primitive Art* (Harmondsworth, 1940): 'Modern art can learn from primitive plastic art, particularly from African sculpture, a refreshing naivete, a wholesome concentration on essentials, and a spontaneous approach to both man and beast . . .' (p145); and 'given the necessary freedom and encouragement, the African is able to take hold of a traditional European craft, and make it into something of his own.' (p149); 'Modern art education has also scored a triumph among the Australian Aborigines.' (p150).

[12] Thomas to Whinnom, 3 October 1938.
[13] *Indigo Days*, op. cit., p95.
[14] *Daily Express*, 18 October 1938.
[15] *Northern Echo*, 17 October 1938.
[16] 'Anyone Can Paint', catalogue (Mansfield etc, 1938).
[17] *News Chronicle*, 31 January 1939.
[18] Ibid.
[19] Letter from Mary Adam to Robert Lyon, copies of scripts, comments by Harry Wilson in the author's possession.
[20] 'Mixing Paints and People', *Morpeth Herald* (nd, 1938).

CHAPTER 7

[1] Elizabeth Sussex, *The Rise and Fall of British Documentary* (California, 1975), p110.
[2] 'Tyneside', *Picture Post*, 17 December 1938.
[3] Interview with the author, 1971.
[4] *The Road to Wigan Pier* (London, 1937), p34.
[5] Interview with the author, 1971.
[6] Mass Observation Archive. Quoted in Stanley, thesis, op. cit.
[7] 'Unprofessional Painting', catalogue, p4.
[8] 'On "Proletarian Art"', *New Britain*, 1, 1934, p32.
[9] G. A. W. Tomlinson, *Coal Miner* (London, 1937), p123.

CHAPTER 8

[1] Arthur Gordon, thesis, 1954.
[2] Interview with the author, 1971.
[3] Letter to exhibition organiser, Whitechapel Art Gallery, 12 April 1973. Dickey may have tutored a class in applied art in 1927/8 but by all accounts other than this letter, Lyon's WEA class was a completely new departure.
[4] Eric Newton, *War Through Artists' Eyes* (London, 1945), p8.
[5] 'The Drawings of Henry Moore' (Tate Gallery, 1977), p37.
[6] Letter to the author, 18 June 1974.
[7] 'Seventeen Adventurers with Brush and Paint', *Morpeth Herald*, 20 June 1941.
[8] Ibid.
[9] Ibid.
[10] Lyon, thesis, op. cit., pp114–15.
[11] Letter in group archive.
[12] Lyon, thesis, op. cit., p118.
[13] Percy Horton, 'The Naive and the Sophisticated', *Left Review*, April 1938.

CHAPTER 9

[1] Letter from Whinnom to William Cookson, 9 April 1943. Group archive.
[2] B. Ivor Evans and Mary Glasgow, *The Arts in England* (London, 1949), p117.
[3] Letters from Sutherland and Moore were shown in the Group's 1973 exhibition at the Whitechapel Art Gallery and subsequently mislaid. In the *Guardian*, 8 April 1973, Caroline Tisdall quoted the letters: 'Graham Sutherland regretted that he was unlikely to make it for some months, and Henry Moore was fully occupied until the following year . . .'
[4] J. B. Pick, *Under the Crust* (London, 1946), p8.
[5] Kilbourn to the author, 12 June 1977. See also Arthur Gordon's thesis, op. cit.
[6] Lyon to Whinnom, 24 April 1945.
[7] James Boswell, *The Artist's Dilemma* (London, 1947), p64.
[8] Interview with the author, 1971.
[9] Lyon to Whinnom, 12 May 1953. Group archive.
[10] *Daily Herald*, 16 February 1948.
[11] *News Chronicle*, 16 February 1948.

CHAPTER 10

[1] Arthur Jeffress to Whinnom, August 1948. Group archive.

[2] Marita Ross, *Everybody's*, 6 November 1948: 'Joseph Nicholson . . . a hefty young steel worker from Seaton Delaval.' Others in the exhibition included Alfred Wallis, Scottie Wilson, 'Douanier' Rousseau and Annie Carline (mother-in-law of Stanley Spencer).
[3] Interview with the author, 1971.
[4] Interview with the author, 1971.
[5] *Ashington and District Advertiser*, 13 July 1951.
[6] 'Where Miners Work Rich Seams of Enlightenment', *Manchester Guardian*, 28 September 1953.
[7] Quoted in N. Gray, Introduction to 'Helen Sutherland Collection' (Arts Council, 1970).
[8] Nicholson to Whinnom, 25 November 1953.
[9] Nicholson to Whinnom, 7 January 1954.
[10] Interview with the author, 1971.
[11] *Newcastle Evening Chronicle*, 13 August 1959.
[12] Sid Chaplin, *The Thin Seam and Other Stories* (London, 1951), p63.
[13] Clancy Sigal, *Weekend in Dinlock* (New York, 1960), p141.

CHAPTER 11

[1] 'Helen Sutherland Collection' (Arts Council, 1970), p5.
[2] This and following quotations from 'Pigeons and Paint', directed by Tristram Powell, BBC, 1972.
[3] Floyd to Lyon nd (January 1972): 'I don't often get the chance to get my paints out, as I have everything to do myself. I'm not grumbling. I only thank my blessings I can manage, but Monday night I was standing thinking in the art gallery that my late wife and you would have been proud to see the results of your and her encouragements.'
[4] *Tribune*, 20 April 1973.
[5] Guy Brett, 'Miners' Paintings Tell a Vivid Story', *The Times*, 10 April 1973.
[6] Ezra to the author, 25 March 1975.
[7] Kilbourn to the author, 4 September 1975.
[8] Other artists included were Illtyd David and Herbert Cooper.
[9] The exhibition went to Utrecht, Tilborg, Arnhem, Amersfoort, Kerkrade, Emmen, Zwolle and Delft.
[10] Also the documentary 'In An Ideal World' (Feaver/Heycock), BBC, 1979, with contributions from Janet Adam Smith, Charles Madge, James Fitton and Pearl Binder.
[11] 'My Life as a Pitman', Introductions by Kilbourn and Feaver (Midland Group, Nottingham, 1977).
[12] 'Peasant Paintings from Hu County, Shansi Province, China', Introduction by Guy Brett (Arts Council, 1976).
[13] Interview with the author, August 1977.
[14] Kilbourn to the author, 9 June 1976.
[15] Interview with the author, August 1977.

CHAPTER 12

[1] Arthur Whinnom, 'Ashington WEA Class – Visit to London', 1936.
[2] The exhibition opened on Saturday 26 April 1980; an accompanying display of photographs of Byker by Sirkka-Liisa Konttinen was also shown. See Feaver, 'How a Colliery Art Class Took Peking By Storm', *Observer Magazine*, 25 October 1980.
[3] See Guy Brett, *Through Our Own Eyes: Popular Art and Modern History* (London, 1987).
[4] The commemorative brochure reproduced *Stonemen Redding Mothergate Canch*, by Oliver Kilbourn. 'For those needing an interpretation of the title, Redding means getting rid of, cleaning up. Mothergate is the main entrance to the coal face. Canch is the roof.'
[5] Notes from Kilbourn to the author, August 1987, January 1988.
[6] David Williams (ed.), 'Northumberland Miners' Banners' (MIDNAG Ashington, 1987).
[7] Kilbourn to the author, 9 June 1976.

Index